Conducting Market Research for International Business

Conducting Market Research for International Business

S. Tamer Cavusgil
Georgia State University

Gary Knight
Florida State University

John Riesenberger
MannKind Corporation

Attila Yaprak
Wayne State University

Conducting Market Research for International Business
Copyright © Business Expert Press, LLC, 2009.

First published in 2009 by
Business Expert Press, LLC
222 East 46th Street, New York, NY 10017
www.businessexpertpress.com

ISBN-13: 978-1-60649-025-9 (paperback)
ISBN-10: 1-60649-025-7 (paperback)

ISBN-13: 978-1-60649-026-6 (e-book)
ISBN-10: 1-60649-026-5 (e-book)

DOI forthcoming.

A publication in the Business Expert Press International Business collection

Collection ISSN (print) forthcoming
Collection ISSN (electronic) forthcoming

Cover design by Artistic Group—Monroe, NY
Interior design by Scribe, Inc.

First edition: January 2009

10 9 8 7 6 5 4 3 2 1

Printed in the United States of America.

Abstract

This book is designed to help managers and scholars understand the fundamentals of international market research. It offers a comprehensive treatment of the research issues that international business managers face when contemplating market entry, engaging buyers in foreign markets, maintaining and growing market share, and expanding to newer opportunities abroad. The book describes how to initiate an international research project—from analyzing the nature and scope of the research to the preliminary stages, gathering data, designing surveys, sampling, analyzing the data, and more. It also provides a sound theoretical base, supported by numerous examples. This practical, detailed guide further offers extensive coverage on using the Internet for research.

Key areas of coverage include the six activities associated with Global Market Opportunity Assessment (GMOA); fundamentals of international market research; the types of information needed in international research, and how these are gathered and converted into useful, managerially relevant information; the merits and limitations of primary and secondary data, and suggestions regarding Internet-based resources; research using primary data, particularly regarding survey research; a three-phased approach for conducting international market research composed of macro-, micro-, and cultural analysis; methodological considerations in international market research, such as validity, reliability, and equivalency in conducting research; specific measurement issues that researchers face in international studies, and methods to overcome these issues; an extended example of a market research situation facing a typical firm; important research issues, such as developing research questions, constructing measures, sampling, and data collection; a listing of numerous Internet sites, organized by category, for conducting research; a sample international business plan and the research requirements for completing such a plan.

Keywords

International marketing research; international market research; international market entry; data collection; Internet-based international market research; Global Market Opportunity Assessment (GMOA); primary and secondary data in international market research; cultural analysis; validity, reliability, and equivalency in international research; international business plan

Contents

Introduction

A fundamental challenge facing internationalizing firms centers on finding solutions to managerial problems in multiple international markets. This challenge is compounded by the need to acquire a substantive understanding of those markets, with a view to achieving satisfactory performance, given a limited base of organizational resources. In this book we offer a comprehensive treatment of the research issues that international business managers face when contemplating market entry, engaging consumers in markets that they have entered, maintaining market share in those markets, growing from those positions, and expanding from those markets to newer opportunities abroad. The book describes how to initiate an international research project—from analyzing the nature and scope of the research, through the preliminary stages of gathering data, designing surveys, sampling, analyzing the data, and more. We also provide a sound theoretical base, supported by numerous examples. This practical and detailed guide further offers extensive coverage on using the Internet for research. We address the most pressing specific issues that confront international marketers in the chapters that follow.

In Chapter 1, we introduce international market research, summarize the characteristics of foreign markets, and highlight the importance of research to ensure international organizational success.

In Chapter 2, we summarize the six activities associated with Global Market Opportunity Assessment (GMOA). Firms regularly encounter favorable combinations of circumstances, locations, or timing that offer prospects for exporting, investing, sourcing, or partnering in foreign markets. GMOA is an approach for analyzing these opportunities in order to choose the most appropriate ones to optimize company performance.

In Chapter 3, we explain the fundamentals of international market research, the types of information needed in international research, and how these are gathered and converted into useful, managerially relevant information. We also address the merits and limitations of primary and secondary data, and offer suggestions regarding online resources. We then discuss the nature of buyer behavior. Finally, in a special section called "Food for Thought," we examine research on perceptions, attitudes, beliefs, and values, all of which strongly influence buyer intentions to purchase.

In Chapter 4, we examine research using primary data, particularly regarding survey research. We also address focus groups and the challenges of conducting these. As Food for Thought, we offer a three-phased approach to conducting international market research composed of macro-, micro-, and cultural analyses. Managers can use this framework to assist in developing a deeper understanding of new markets or markets where they are operating now.

In Chapter 5, we address methodological considerations in international market research. We highlight the challenges of research validity, reliability, and equivalency in developing measures and assessing constructs. We highlight the institutional environment in which international market research takes place. As Food for Thought, we offer a deeper discussion of some of the measurement issues that researchers face in international studies, especially survey research in multiple countries. We offer coping mechanisms that help to overcome these issues.

In Chapter 6, we present an extended example of a market research situation involving Acme Motor Company, based in the United States. Acme seeks to market its line of fuel-efficient automobiles to France and other countries in Europe. We weave into this example important research issues, such as properly modeling the research question, developing hypotheses, constructing the relative measures, and sampling and data collection. We also address data analysis through research methods and reporting research findings in a managerially relevant manner. We hope that you will find this book to be a practical, detailed, and useful guide to international marketing research.

CHAPTER 1

Understanding Markets Through International Market Research

International Business: An Introduction

International business is the performance of trade and foreign direct investment activities across national borders. The pace of international business has greatly accelerated in recent years. Companies are increasingly marketing their offerings in foreign countries. Much of this heightened activity is the result of various forces collectively termed "globalization." Broadly, globalization refers to the growing economic integration and interdependency of countries worldwide. Globalization has coincided with massive growth in international transactions. For example, in 1960 international trade worldwide was modest—about $100 billion per year. Today it accounts for a huge proportion of the world economy, amounting to some $10 trillion annually. There are more opportunities to market products internationally than ever before.

Going international has also gotten easier. A few decades ago, international business was dominated by large, multinational companies. Today, largely thanks to globalization and advanced information and communication technologies, companies of all sizes regularly market their offerings around the world. The number of firms doing international business has grown enormously.

For simplicity's sake, in this book we discuss international business mainly in terms of *companies* that market *products* in foreign countries. However, the concepts described here apply equally to the marketing of services, capital, technology, know-how, and even nations themselves.

Services are the fastest growing sector in international business and include offerings such as architecture, construction, and engineering services; banking and various financial services; education, management training, and technical training; movies, music, and Internet-based entertainment; data processing and other information services; professional business services; transportation; travel, hospitality, and tourism; and retailing of all kinds.

International business is also often undertaken by governments and public agencies. The concepts described in this book apply to these entities as well. In short, all kinds of organizations are marketing a wide range of offerings abroad, from industrial machinery to the latest clothing fashions, from financial services to managerial know-how.

Companies undertake international business for a variety of reasons, including the ability to

- seek growth via market diversification;
- earn higher profits from lucrative foreign markets;
- better serve existing customers who have located abroad;
- gain economies of scale in production and marketing;
- amortize the costs of product development and marketing across many markets;
- obtain new product ideas from foreign settings; and
- confront competitors more effectively in competitors' home markets.

Historically, the most popular markets for international business were advanced economy countries in North America and Europe, as well as Australia, New Zealand, and Japan. Today firms increasingly target "emerging markets," such as Brazil, China, India, Mexico, and Saudi Arabia. There are substantial market opportunities even in developing economies in Africa, Latin America, and Southeast Asia. The attractiveness of emerging markets arises primarily from growing affluence in these countries.

Compared to doing business in one's home country, international business is characterized by four major types of risk in foreign markets.

Figure 1.1
The four risks in foreign markets

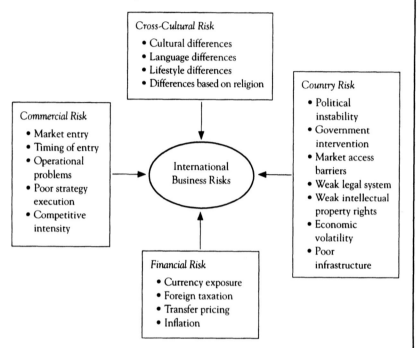

1. Initially, foreign markets are subject to *cross-cultural risk*, which refers to substantial differences in language, lifestyles, mindsets, customs, and religions of people living abroad. Each country's historic, ethnic, geographic, and religious circumstances lead its citizens to consume according to established patterns. For example, when shopping for food, people may shop daily, instead of weekly, a pattern that affects product size, package design, pricing, and distribution, among other factors.

2. *Country risk* (also known as *political risk*) refers to the potentially adverse effects on company activities caused by developments in political, legal, and economic environments abroad. Governments frequently intervene in firms' marketing activities, for example, by restricting access to markets or imposing bureaucratic procedures. Countries may have weak legal systems or underdeveloped intellectual property rights. Economic conditions, such as inflation and government indebtedness, can pose substantial challenges. Foreign

buyers have varying income levels, which may restrict their purchasing power. Infrastructure needed to market products and services, such as transportation networks and communications systems, may be lacking.

3. Countries are subject to *financial risk*, which often includes adverse fluctuations in currency exchange rates. These fluctuations can strongly influence company pricing strategy and consequent sales. Other potential challenges include the level of taxation. Income, value-added, and sales taxes vary substantially from country to country. Transfer pricing can be complicated by exchange rates, currency restrictions, and income repatriation laws. Some countries suffer from high or varying inflation levels, which complicate the firms' pricing activities.

4. *Commercial risk* refers to the potential loss or failure that result from business strategies, tactics, or procedures that are poorly developed or poorly executed. Managers may make poor choices in market entry, pricing, creation of product features, and promotional themes. Management must orchestrate the operational dimensions of market entry, such as logistics, customs clearance, and local distribution. The firm must account for foreign competitors and competitive intensity in the target market. While such concerns also exist in the domestic market, their occurrence is usually more pronounced or more complex in foreign markets.

The four types of risks are ever present and usually cannot be avoided. However, with proper international market research, they can be anticipated and managed.

Companies enter foreign markets via various *entry modes*:

- *Exporting* refers to sales of products or services to customers located abroad from a base in the home country or from a third country.
- *Foreign direct investment* refers to the securing of ownership of assets located abroad, such as a factory or a marketing subsidiary.
- *Collaborative ventures* include joint ventures in which the firm

also obtains ownership of foreign assets abroad, but in partnership with one or more other firms.

- *Licensing* occurs when the firm allows a foreign partner to use its intellectual property in return for royalties or other compensation.
- *Franchising* is an advanced form of licensing in which the firm allows a foreign partner to use an entire business system, in exchange for royalties and other compensation.

Each foreign market entry mode has advantages and disadvantages, and each places specific demands on the firm's managerial and financial resources. Each entails a distinctive approach to marketing activities. Managers usually consider six major variables when selecting an entry mode:

1. the *goals and objectives* of the firm, such as desired profitability, market share, or competitive positioning;
2. the financial, organizational, and technological *resources and capabilities* available to the firm;
3. *unique conditions* in the target country, such as legal, cultural, and economic circumstances, as well as the nature of business infrastructure, such as distribution and transportation systems;
4. *risks* inherent in each proposed foreign venture in relation to the firm's goals and objectives in pursuing internationalization;
5. the nature and extent of *competition* from existing rivals and from companies that may enter the market later; and
6. the characteristics of the *product or service* to be offered to customers in the market.

What Is International Market Research?

Each of the risks and business approaches highlighted in the previous sections influences the nature of the firm's international business activities. The complexities of doing business abroad necessitate performing international market research and acquiring competitive intelligence. International market research is the systematic design, collection, analysis, and reporting of findings relevant to a specific business decision facing the company, and it involves at least one foreign market. Competitive intelligence refers to collecting and analyzing data and information about a company's current and potential competitors and recommending actionable business decisions. Experienced international firms conduct research to forecast potential risks, understand their implications, and take proactive steps to minimize the damage that they can do. Firms also conduct research to better understand foreign customers, competitors, and general environments in foreign target markets.

Research is the foundation of marketing decision making. Indeed, many firms regard research as a key ingredient in gaining an advantage over competitors. For this reason, sophisticated managers are on a constant quest to acquire large amounts of customer, competitive, and market information. Information technologies and the Internet greatly assist in the information gathering process. Internationally, the Internet offers an unparalleled ability to track and monitor customers. Search engines, tools for conducting online surveys, and access to large databases containing secondary research are among the various ways in which the Internet facilitates international market research. In many ways, information and Internet-based technologies have leveled the research playing field, allowing even small companies to acquire high-quality data on international markets.

Research helps the manager acquire a deeper understanding of foreign markets and develop strategies and tactics needed for successful international business operations. Consider a company's need for objective information about a new market. How much do you know about the geography, culture, economy, and commercial environment of countries other than your own? How well informed are you about market entry and business operations in individual foreign markets?

Recently, Research In Motion (RIM), the firm that makes the Black-Berry brand of personal e-mail devices, has been expanding in the rapidly growing emerging market of India, whose population is about one billion people. What kind of international market research does RIM need in order to arrive at a sound and realistic decision about its prospects there? Among other things, RIM needs to explore consumer and household

characteristics and preferences about personal communications via wireless devices, shopping behavior with respect to such devices, potential interest in the various BlackBerry models that RIM offers, the availability and capabilities of local wireless device retailers, and the nature and intensity of competition.

In the run-up to internationalization, most managers start out with a limited knowledge of the countries in which they wish to do business. Yet foreign markets entail very different conditions than those in the firm's home market. International business poses substantial risk and uncertainty. To succeed and avoid blunders, managers must develop a thorough understanding of each target market. Managers must understand customer and competitor characteristics before committing significant resources. They must acquire a range of information and insights through formal market research and gathering competitive intelligence (Lim, Sharkey, & Kim, 1996). Acting in the absence of adequate knowledge can be costly in terms of resources and reputation. There is no substitute for informed decision making in international business. Market research investigates both organizations and people using techniques based in the social sciences, in fields such as economics, sociology, and psychology. Social science researchers use tried-and-true scientific methods.

Table 1.1   Typical Research Projects in International Business

WHEN THE BUSINESS DECISION INVOLVES	THE FIRM SHOULD CONDUCT RESEARCH ON AREAS SUCH AS
what markets to target	nature of cultural, legal, and economic environment in various potential markets; size of markets; level of product demand in markets; customer characteristics; buyer behavior; requirements for achieving customer satisfaction; and extent and nature of competition
how the product should be developed or adapted	nature of customers in target market, characteristics of products sought, positioning the product, choosing a brand name, enhancing brand preference, nature of product packaging, and extent and nature of competition
how to market the product	nature of cultural, legal, and economic environment; developing advertising copy; developing sales promotion techniques; compensating the sales force; types of media to use; and how to differentiate the product from competitors' offerings
how to price the product	price elasticity of demand, optimal price setting, and discount options
how to distribute the product	availability and quality of distributors, distributor interest, shipping options, and retail store site selection

Table 1.1 presents a sampling of research that firms undertake in international business.

The Benefits of International Market Research

Understanding foreign markets is important for various reasons:

1. *Forecasting.* Research yields a set of assumptions about the future that are critical to managerial decision making. Most strategic decisions in companies are based on an extensive set of assumptions about the future. For example, firms forecast demand for products in new markets. As the future becomes the present, many of these assumptions prove to be inaccurate or false. Research provides timely reports and recommendations that can assist in updating these assumptions and aid executive management in strategic decision making about current and future value-chain activities. Research also helps with "hypothesis testing"—that is, assessing theories or "gut feelings" that the firm may hold regarding particular issues. For example, the manager may suspect that there is a difference between the purchasing habits of one type of customer as compared to another type, a question that can be addressed via hypothesis testing.

2. *Planning.* Research helps managers to formulate sound international business plans. Managers become aware of challenges, risks, and potentially insurmountable problems and can therefore make sound decisions and develop appropriate strategies and tactics. Research helps to identify and describe in detail problems and challenges facing the firm. For example, during the planning process, international research helps firms to identify target markets and market segments more skillfully; position products relative to competitors; develop branding strategy more effectively; and devise other strategic and tactical actions that translate into marketing the right product, at the right price, using the right communications, via the right distribution channels.

3. *Competitive intelligence.* Research should aim to track and assess each current and potential competitor's strengths, weaknesses, opportunities, and threats. Intelligence about competitors' product offerings, pricing practices, and distribution patterns helps the firm to

develop its own strategic responses. The researcher should focus on areas where competitors can threaten the success of a proposed foreign venture. Such knowledge aids in the development of offerings and approaches that differentiate the firm in the market. It facilitates the design of strategies and tactics that take competitor activities into account and maximize the likelihood of the firm's international business success. Information about competitors is generally obtained through publicly available documents, such as brochures, the Internet, and the library.

4. *Monitor progress on organizational objectives.* Skillful research helps managers to better understand the extent to which company objectives are being achieved and what course corrections, if any, are needed in order to ensure success for many years to come. For example, managers want to know the extent to which the firm is reaching profit or market-share goals in foreign markets. Research helps firms to assess the effectiveness of their strategies and tactics regarding value-chain activities, such as production and marketing.

5. *Increase organizational skill and knowledge base.* As they research foreign markets, managers increase the skills that they need for interacting and negotiating with the various associates, partners, and customers whom they encounter as they deepen international involvements. Strong marketing skills are important competitive advantages that increase organizational performance. In addition, research leads to knowledge that grows over time, becoming an integral part of the organization's collective wisdom. Unlike most other corporate resources that are depleted when used, market research accumulates with ongoing sharing and usage. The sharing of knowledge enriches all users and leads to better decision making within the firm, increasing the likelihood of international business success.

Two Examples

When Procter & Gamble initially launched Pampers disposable diapers in Japan some years ago, managers did not understand key characteristics of Japanese households and how Japanese parents take care of their babies. Most young families in Japan live in small homes and lack the space to store big boxes of diapers. Mothers in Japan change their babies' diapers about twice as often as mothers in the United States and do not need the thick diapers favored by U.S. mothers. After Procter & Gamble conducted the appropriate research and understood these basic facts, managers redesigned the product and marketing effort, and Pampers became the biggest-selling brand in Japan.

Samsung, the South Korean electronics manufacturer, used international market research proactively to forecast and create offerings that have helped to make Samsung the world leader in several product categories (UNCTAD, 2006). In the 1990s, Samsung managers conducted comprehensive market research to develop a plan to remake Samsung into a "global brand," emphasizing sophisticated marketing strategies. These efforts helped the firm to become the world's leading marketer of flat screen TVs and other electronics, surpassing industry giants Sony and Motorola. From its lackluster image in the 1990s, Samsung today has acquired capabilities for developing and marketing state-of-the-art products. Recently, Samsung established 10 research and development (R&D) centers around the world that drive the development of technologies in digital media and appliances, telecommunications, and semiconductors, emphasizing designs and features that enjoy widespread popularity. Research laid the foundation for Samsung to develop sophisticated branding strategies and incorporate originality, convenience, fashion, and user-friendliness into products that have achieved substantial market share worldwide (Kiley, 2007).

Challenges of International Market Research

International market research entails a range of complex activities. Gathering accurate and reliable information is complicated by cross-national differences in language, culture, laws and regulations, and income levels and other socioeconomic conditions. In addition, desired information is often unavailable, unreliable, or expressed in abstract measurement units.

For example, in Asia, Citibank markets its credit cards across a range of countries such as China, India, Indonesia, Japan, Malaysia, and Singapore. Each of these countries has a distinctive banking infrastructure, commercial practices, attitudes toward money and credit, and, where

Islam is practiced, restrictions on paying interest. Within each country, attitudes and practices vary substantially between urban and rural dwellers.

In its efforts to market food products worldwide, Nestlé must acquire a thorough understanding of what consumers regard as tasty food, where they shop for it, and how far they are willing to travel to obtain it. They must consider buyer preferences regarding package design, serving size, and ease of preparation, as well as the constellation of values, attitudes, and beliefs that lead consumers to choose one food product over another. They must acquire knowledge about how best to design marketing variables—product features, pricing, communications, and distribution channels—and how these variables interact. All of these factors must be considered in light of their effect on the marketing and perceptions of existing Nestlé and competing products. Research must also attempt to forecast trends and shifts in market segments for the long term.

International market research is a necessary yet substantial undertaking. Much of the data must be meticulously and thoroughly acquired in the field, as broad-based information gathered from public sources such as libraries and the Internet are insufficient for providing the in-depth knowledge that the firm needs to succeed. The firm faces a trade-off between doing research correctly and the resources (especially time and money) needed to perform the research. Management must find the right balance between its need for comprehensive and relevant information and the costs involved in conducting the research. In the new millennium, exploring and developing new market opportunities abroad is one of the most demanding, yet the most rewarding, economic activities. Pursuit of international opportunities can be possible only through ready access to, and sophisticated interpretation of, information about foreign markets. The remaining chapters of this book are devoted to making this type of understanding possible.

CHAPTER 2

Global Market Opportunity Assessment

Making good choices determines the success of entry and operations in foreign markets. Good decision making hinges on obtaining information about which products and services to offer and where and how to offer them. The more you know about an opportunity, the better equipped you will be to exploit it. Data and information on business opportunities are particularly critical in international markets, which are characterized by substantial uncertainty and risk.

Central to research success is identifying and defining the most promising business opportunities abroad. A global market opportunity is a favorable combination of circumstances, locations, or timing that offers prospects for exporting, investing, sourcing, or partnering in foreign markets (Cavusgil et al., 2008). Companies regularly encounter opportunities to sell their offerings, establish factories or other production facilities, procure input goods, or enter rewarding collaborative ventures in markets all around the world. Global market opportunities hold the prospect of enhancing company performance, often far beyond what the firm can achieve in the home market. In the sections that follow, for simplicity's sake, we will discuss global market opportunities mainly in terms of exporting and marketing products abroad. However, the discussion applies equally to opportunities for investing, sourcing, or partnering as well.

Global Market Opportunity Assessment (GMOA) is the process of analyzing company readiness to internationalize, assessing the suitability of products and services for foreign markets, screening countries for entry, assessing market and sales potential in identified countries, and choosing qualified business partners in the target markets. In this chapter, we discuss six sequential activities that comprise GMOA that firms should undertake in order to define and pursue global market opportunities. These activities, and their associated rationale and typical tasks, are represented in Table 2.1 (Cavusgil et al., 2008).

As reflected in the table, the following are the six activities:

1. Analyze organizational readiness to internationalize.
2. Assess suitability of products and services for foreign markets.
3. Screen countries to identify attractive target markets.
4. Assess industry market potential, or market demand, for the product or service.
5. Select qualified business partners, such as suppliers or distributors.
6. Estimate company sales potential for each target market.

We will now examine in detail the six activities identified in Table 2.1 (Cavusgil, Knight, & Riesenberger, 2008).

Activity One: Analyze Organizational Readiness to Internationalize

Before investing in a substantial international venture, whether it involves launching a product abroad or sourcing from a foreign supplier, the firm must conduct a formal assessment of its readiness to internationalize. The evaluation is critical for international success, for experienced and inexperienced firms alike. The analysis is similar to a SWOT analysis, in which management evaluates the firm's own Strengths and Weaknesses, as well as Opportunities and Threats in the business environment. At this stage, the firm examines itself to ascertain the degree to which it has the motivation, resources, and competencies necessary to successfully undertake international business. The firm also conducts formal research on the opportunities and threats that it faces in the markets where it wants to do business. For example, managers research the specific needs and wants of buyers, as well as the nature of competing products and the risks involved in the target market.

The goal of analyzing organizational readiness to internationalize is to ascertain what resources the firm has, and what resources it needs to develop, that will be sufficient for successful international operations.

Table 2.1   *Global Market Opportunity Assessment: Key Activities*

ACTIVITY	RATIONALE	TYPICAL TASKS
1. Analyze organizational readiness to internationalize	Provides an objective assessment of the firm's preparedness to undertake an international business activity.	List the firm's strengths and weaknesses, as well as recommendations for addressing resource deficiencies and other shortcomings that can hinder achieving company goals abroad.
2. Assess the suitability of the firm's products and services for foreign markets	Provides a systematic assessment of the suitability of the firm's products and services for international customers.	Evaluate the degree of fit between the given product or service and customer needs and characteristics in the target market.
3. Screen countries to identify target markets	Reduces the number of countries that warrant in-depth investigation to a manageable few. This helps ensure that organizational resources are used efficiently and lessens the complexity of the assessment task.	Identify five or six high-potential countries that are most promising for the firm. Consider market size, market-growth rate, market intensity (i.e., buying power of the residents in terms of income level), consumption capacity (i.e., size and growth rate of the country's middle class), infrastructure appropriate for doing business, degree of economic freedom and political risk, and other appropriate variables.
4. Assess industry market potential	Allows the manager to gain an understanding of the *total potential sales* of a product or service in a given foreign market.	Estimate the most likely share of industry sales in each target country. The unit of analysis is the firm's specific industry. Accordingly, investigate and evaluate industry-level barriers to market entry. Develop a 3- to 5-year forecast of industry sales in the market. Identify market-entry barriers. Examine key variables such as market size, market growth rate, and trends in the industry. Assess the nature of competitors in the market. Investigate the degree of industry-specific protectionism. Analyze standards and regulations that apply to the firm's products. Evaluate the availability and sophistication of distribution infrastructure in the marketplace, appropriate for the firm's industry.
5. Select foreign business partners	Collaborating with suitable partners helps the firm achieve its goals in foreign markets. This stage helps ensure that the manager identifies and decides on the most appropriate partners.	Prepare a "wish list" of ideal partner qualifications, such as the value-adding activities required of foreign business partners, desirable attributes in foreign business partners, and the nature of activities that the partners will perform.

(*continued on next page*)

Table 2.1   Global Market Opportunity Assessment: Key Activities (continued)

ACTIVITY	RATIONALE	TYPICAL TASKS
6. Estimate company sales potential	Allows the manager to develop a reliable forecast of the most likely share of sales that the firm can achieve during a given period in the particular market of interest.	Develop a 3- to 5-year forecast of company sales in the target market. The unit of analysis is the specific market(s) that the firm is targeting. Acquire an understanding of factors that influence company sales potential and estimate the ability of the firm to sell its products in the market. Examine the capabilities of partners, available distribution channels, the level of competition, appropriate pricing schemes, and the risk tolerance of upper management for foreign market entry.

Factors to consider include the goals and objectives that management envisions for internationalization; the extent of the firm's international experience; the skills, capabilities, and resources available for internationalization; and the nature of support available from the firm's network of relationships. If as a result of this self-assessment, management discovers that the firm lacks key resources, it must acquire these resources and make any other preparations before allowing the venture to go forward.

In conducting this type of analysis, it is useful to ask the following types of questions:

- What does the firm hope to gain from the international venture? For some companies, the main goal might be to increase sales or profits. For others, the goal might be to reduce costs—for example, by moving manufacturing to a foreign location.
- Is the contemplated international venture consistent with other company goals, now or in the future? Any venture should be undertaken in the context of the firm's mission and overall strategic plans. Over time, various opportunities present themselves. The firm cannot pursue them all. Management must identify those that generate optimal benefits and make best use of company resources.
- What demands will the venture place on company resources, such as managerial time, personnel, and finance, as well as production and marketing capacity? Management must confirm

that it has sufficient resources to carry the project to successful fruition.

- What is the source of the firm's competitive advantages? Here managers evaluate the reasons for company success. Competitive advantage derives from doing things better than competitors and is typically based on strong research and development (R&D), superior sourcing, competent production activities, skillful marketing, very effective distribution, or other value-chain activities in which the firm demonstrates substantial prowess. It is important to understand what advantages the firm has, so that these can be leveraged for maximal performance abroad.

Organizational readiness assessment is an ongoing process. Managers should continuously verify the firm's ability to perform in ways that maximize outcomes in foreign markets. Managers can use diagnostic tools to facilitate a self-audit of readiness to internationalize, such as CORE™ (Company Readiness to Export), an expert system located at globalEDGE™ (www.globalEDGE.msu.edu). CORE™ asks managers questions about their motivation, skills, and other organizational resources to arrive at an objective assessment of the firm's readiness to venture abroad.

Activity Two: Assess Suitability of Products and Services for Foreign Markets

The next step in GMOA analysis is to acquire an understanding of the degree to which the firm's products and services are appropriate for foreign markets. Products suited for foreign markets typically have one or more of the following characteristics:

- *Sell well in the home market.* Offerings that are popular in the domestic market often succeed abroad as well.
- *Cater to universal needs.* For example, people around the world have similar health concerns, and most demand "everyday" products such as personal care products.
- *Address a need not well served in the foreign market.* Such needs are particularly common in emerging markets and developing

economies. For example, in many African countries people often cannot readily access clean drinking water.

- *Address a new or emergent need abroad.* For example, a tsunami in Indonesia can trigger an urgent need for portable housing. The recent popularity of cell phones in developing economies has stimulated a desire for services that can be offered via cell phones.

Managers need to address other issues as well. When investigating foreign markets for sales of a particular product or service, it is useful to ascertain who initiates purchase of the good, who actually uses it, why people would typically buy it, and where they would buy it. The firm should also find out what economic, cultural, geographic, and other factors in the target market can limit sales. One of the simplest ways to ascertain if an offering holds promise in a given market is to ask potential intermediaries in the market about their views on the product's sales potential. It is also useful to find out if, or to what extent, the product is currently being consumed in the target market and how this consumption has evolved over time. Ultimately, management will want to ascertain how much of the product is made locally, how much is imported, and how much is exported.

In order to gain a sense of a product's usage and popularity, it is useful to attend an industry trade show in the target market and interview prospective distributors and customers. Trade shows often cover entire regions, such as Europe or South America, and this approach provides a means to quickly find out about demand for a product and how it is viewed and used across several markets simultaneously.

Activity Three: Screen Countries to Identify Target Markets

There are more than 200 countries worldwide. It is generally not possible to target them all, and thus management needs to narrow the list of potential markets to the most promising ones. Exporting firms generally prefer countries with low trade barriers, qualified intermediaries, and reliable marketing infrastructure. For companies that outsource value-chain activities, management must choose the most appropriate supplier countries. For companies contemplating foreign direct investment (FDI), it is best to emphasize low-risk countries that promise strong profitability and long-term growth.

Experienced international marketers examine trade statistics that reveal exports and imports in the product category (or a closely related category) by country in order to ascertain which markets are largest and have the best growth profiles. Such statistics are available from the United Nations (UN) and the World Bank, as well as from national government agencies such as the U.S. Department of Commerce and Statistics Canada. Governments regularly publish reports on such topics as "The Construction Products Market in India," "The Market for Automotive Parts in Europe," and the "Country Commercial Guide for Argentina." Often, such reports can be accessed via the Internet.

Failure to choose the right market will result in substantial unrecoverable expenses, opportunity costs, and possible collapse of the venture. When entry is via an expensive mode such as FDI, not choosing the right market is even more costly. Management must choose countries that offer the best prospects, given the firm's particular needs and circumstances. There are two basic methods for accomplishing this: (a) gradual elimination and (b) indexing and ranking.

A researcher who uses the gradual elimination approach begins with a large number of prospective target countries and gradually narrows them down by examining increasingly specific information. The goal is to reduce the number of countries that warrant in-depth investigation as potential targets to a manageable few—for example, five or six. Because research is expensive and time consuming, the researcher should emphasize the most attractive markets. Initially, the researcher obtains information on macro-level market-potential indicators, such as population- and income-related measures, to reduce the number of countries under investigation to a manageable number. Next the researcher examines more specific and precise indicators to narrow the choices. For example, the researcher may inspect current import statistics of the product in each of the short-listed countries to determine the desirability of each market. Most countries record the flow of imported and exported products in order to impose tariffs and other taxes on goods flowing across their national borders. Such statistics are available from international agencies, such as the UN (www.comtrade.un.org/db/) and the Organization for Economic Cooperation and Development (OECD; www.oecd.org).

The second method for choosing the most promising foreign markets is indexing and ranking (Cavusgil, 1997). Using this approach, the researcher assigns scores to countries based on their overall attractiveness. For each country, the researcher first identifies the most appropriate market-potential variables for his or her needs. The researcher then assigns a value to each potential country, representing its relative "score" on each variable. The researcher can also assign weights to each variable to establish its relative importance. The more important the variable, the greater is its weight. The weighted scores are then used to rank the countries.

For example, suppose the researcher has identified the following variables as especially important for assessing initial market potential: market size, market growth rate, and political stability. He or she would next obtain data for each of these variables for a collection of countries that seem initially promising. In the early stages, market size may be measured by looking up the population of each country. By itself, however, a large population is insufficient. The market should also be growing at a significant rate, in terms of population or income.

Countries with strong income growth are desirable targets. For example, the researcher would typically examine population, national income, and income growth for each of the previous 4 or 5 years. Examining the trend line of these variables gives a good indication of each country's sales prospects. For many consumer products, the firm will want to target the "middle class" in each country, as it is typically the largest and, in aggregate, the wealthiest class in most countries. For example, even though China and India are poor countries, the middle class in each of these countries now represents more than 200 million people. When compared to affluent countries in Europe, which internationalizing firms have historically targeted, China and India now represent very sizable and promising markets.

A recent ranking (globalEDGE™, 2005) of attractive markets based on several variables categorized China in first place in terms of market size but very low in terms of "economic freedom" and "infrastructure." Accordingly, there are always trade-offs in targeting country markets. No single country is attractive on all dimensions. The researcher must contend with less desirable features alongside more desirable features. In contrast to China, Singapore scores well in terms of economic freedom, but its population is small. India scores well in terms of economic growth but suffers from poor marketing infrastructure.

Country rankings are not static. They evolve over time due to shifting economic events, emergent technologies, or country-specific developments. Thus, a country that is unattractive today might become very attractive in a few years. For example, some years ago Ireland was a relatively unattractive investment destination. However, thanks to government policies that promote investment and entrepreneurship, as well as the emergence of the European Union (EU), Ireland in recent years has become a very attractive investment destination, particularly for firms seeking to build factories that serve the large EU marketplace.

Once the researcher has identified a set of attractive country markets, the next step is to narrow the focus by investigating more specific variables relative to each potential market. The nature of variables to consider usually varies by industry. When researching the market for soft drinks, for example, the researcher might investigate the number of young people in each country and the quality and extent of retailing infrastructure sufficient for soft drink sales. In the medical equipment industry, for each country, the researcher would gather data on health care expenditures, number of physicians per capita, and number of hospital beds per capita. Firms in the banking industry would seek data on commercial risk and interest fluctuations over time.

In addition, depending on the industry, researchers will usually apply different weights to each market potential variable. For example, in the leisure boating industry, population size is relatively less important than in the footwear industry, where population can be a very important indicator. Each firm must identify the most important variables that suit its circumstances and assign appropriate weights to each variable.

Screening Countries for Global Sourcing and Direct Investment

In addition to exporting, firms undertake other entry modes, such as sourcing to obtain inputs from foreign suppliers or FDI to set up production and assembly facilities abroad. While the basic goals of GMOA remain the same when employing other entry modes, the researcher may use a different set of criteria for screening countries. We now turn to the specific aspects of screening associated with FDI and global sourcing.

FDI represents a long-term investment in a foreign country in order to build or acquire physical assets, such as a factory or a marketing subsidiary. The types of variables to consider when undertaking FDI usually differ from those examined for entry via exporting. For example, as FDI often implies setting up a factory, the availability in the target market of skilled labor and managerial talent are relatively important. The researcher typically considers such variables as the following:

- *country risk*, including regulatory, political, economic, and cultural barriers, and the legal environment for protecting company assets;
- *government incentives*, such as the availability of low-interest loans, tax holidays, subsidized training, or direct grants;
- *long-term growth prospects* in the target country;
- *cost of doing business*, including rates for wages and taxes, the cost and availability of commercial infrastructure, and access to skilled workers, as well as capital markets; and
- *competitive environment*, including the intensity of competition from local and foreign firms.

There are various sources of publicly available information useful for assisting in screening for FDI. For example, the FDI Indices methodology provided by the United Nations Conference on Trade and Development (UNCTAD, available at www.unctad.org) benchmarks both FDI performance and potential and ranks countries by how well they perform as recipients or originators of FDI. The Foreign Direct Investment Confidence Index, provided annually by the consulting firm A. T. Kearney (www.atkearney.com), tracks the FDI intentions of the world's top firms based on political, economic, and regulatory circumstances in each of numerous countries.

When the firm screens countries to find the best locations for global sourcing, management is concerned with the procurement of finished products, intermediate goods, and services from suppliers located abroad. Sourcing is vital to most firms, including those whose main offering is services. The types of screening variables to consider for global sourcing include the cost and quality of inputs, stability of exchange rates, reliability of suppliers, and the presence of a work force with superior technical skills. The consultancy A. T. Kearney (www.atkearney.com) prepares an annual Offshore Location Attractiveness Index that supports managers in understanding and comparing the factors that make countries attractive as potential locations for offshoring of service activities such as information technology, business processes, and call centers.

When A. T. Kearney evaluates countries, it accounts for three major dimensions:

1. *financial structure*, which includes compensation costs (e.g., average wages), infrastructure costs (e.g., electricity and telecommunications systems), and tax and regulatory costs (e.g., tax burden, corruption, and fluctuating exchange rates);
2. *people skills and availability* account for a suppliers' experience and skills, labor-force availability, education and linguistic proficiency, and employee-attrition rates; and
3. *business environment* assesses economic and political aspects of the country.

These are all useful variables to consider when undertaking global sourcing activities.

Activity Four: Assess Industry Market Potential

Once the number of potential countries has been reduced to a manageable number—say five or six—the next step in GMOA is to conduct an in-depth analysis of each of these country markets. In this stage, rather than examining broad, macro-level indicators, the researcher narrows the focus to industry-level market potential indicators. In particular, the researcher estimates the current and future levels of sales expected for the particular industry as a whole. Industry market potential represents an estimate of the likely sales that can be expected for all firms in the particular industry for a specified period of time. Industry market potential is an aggregate of the sales that theoretically could be realized by all companies in the industry. Industry market potential is distinguished from company sales potential in that the latter refers to the share of industry sales that the firm itself expects to achieve during a given time period. Most firms forecast sales at least 3 years into the future for both industry market potential and company sales potential.

Estimating industry market potential helps the researcher to identify the most attractive countries for the firm's products or services. Close examination of country-level characteristics at this stage helps management to decide which countries to retain for subsequent analysis of company sales potential. In addition to gaining industry-specific insights into the markets of interest, managers begin to develop an understanding of the degree to which the firm needs to adapt its product and marketing approaches.

Typical variables to consider include market size, growth rate, and trends *in the specific industry*; industry-specific tariff and nontariff trade barriers; standards and regulations that affect the industry; availability and sophistication of distribution infrastructure appropriate for the industry; and specific customer characteristics and preferences. In addition to generic determinants of demand, each industry sector has its own indicators or distinctive drivers of demand. Marketers of skiwear, for example, examine climate-related factors, such as the average number of snowy days in a typical year. Pharmaceutical firms obtain data on the number of people afflicted with a particular ailment, as well as the level of governmental expenditures on health care. Managers also evaluate factors that affect the marketing and use of the product, such as consumer characteristics, culture, distribution channels, and business practices.

Practical Methods for Assessing Industry Market Potential

Managers use the following practical methods for estimating industry market potential (Cavusgil, 1985):

- *Attend international trade shows.* Industry trade fairs and exhibitions are excellent venues to obtain information on potential markets. By attending a trade fair in the target country, the researcher can learn a great deal about market characteristics that support estimating industry sales potential. Trade fairs are also helpful for identifying potential distributors and other business partners.

- *Ask supplier networks.* Many suppliers serve multiple clients and can be a major source of information about competitors. Firms can gain valuable leads from current suppliers by inquiring of them about competitor activities.

- *Monitor key industry-specific indicators.* The researcher examines specific industry drivers of market demand by collecting data from a variety of sources. For example, Komatsu, a manufacturer of earthmoving equipment, examines the volume of announced construction projects, number of issued building permits, growth rate of households, infrastructure development, and other pertinent indicators to anticipate sales of its construction equipment.

- *Monitor key competitors.* To gain insights into the potential of a particular country, the researcher investigates the degree of major competitor activity in the countries of interest. For example, if Komatsu is considering Russia as a potential market, the researcher investigates the current involvement in Russia of its number one competitor, Caterpillar.

- *Perform simple trend analysis.* This method quantifies the total likely amount of industry market potential by examining aggregate production for the industry as a whole by adding imports from abroad and deducting exports. This gives a rough estimate of the size of the current industry sales in the country.

Data Sources

For each country, the researcher seeks data that directly or indirectly report levels of industry sales and production, as well as the intensity of exports and imports in the product category of interest. One useful data source for this is the National Trade Data Bank (NTDB), available from the U.S. Department of Commerce's STAT-USA and www.export.gov databases (U.S. Department of Commerce, 1992). Specific reports available from the NTDB include

- *Best Market Reports*, which identify the top 10 country markets for specific industry sectors;
- *Country Commercial Guides*, which analyze countries' economic and commercial environments;
- *Industry Sector Analysis Reports*, which analyze market potential for individual industrial sectors; and
- *International Market Insight Reports*, which cover country- and product-specific topics, providing various ideas for approaching markets of interest.

Frequently, data are not available, and the researcher must obtain information indirectly. The researcher may need to be creative and consult any resource that can shed light on the task at hand. Statistics available from national governments are often incomplete, inaccurate, out of date, or stated in units that do not address the firm's immediate needs. Consider the case of a company that sells components in the cellular telecommunications industry. Suppose this firm wants to enter the Japanese market and needs to estimate industry-wide demand. Its researchers consult numerous sources, including reports by the International Telecommunications Union, the NTDB, and several UN publications. Managers investigate the size of the Japanese middle class and its average income, the nature of support infrastructure for cellular systems in Japan, and the nature and number of retail stores that handle cell phones. The researcher also uncovers statistics from the National Telecommunications Trade Association on the number of competitors already active in Japan and their approximate sales volumes. From these sources, the firm can arrive at a rough estimate of market size for cellular telephones and prevailing prices in Japan.

Activity Five: Select Foreign Business Partners

Once a target market has been selected, the next major activity in GMOA is to decide on the types of partners the firm needs for the foreign venture. Business partners are vital to international business success. Partners include such entities as distribution-channel intermediaries and suppliers, as well as collaborative venture partners, such as joint venture partners and franchisees. Firms collaborate for various reasons, generally with the aim of pooling resources, sharing costs, or pursuing goals that one firm on its own cannot achieve.

Companies must exercise great care when choosing partners. To this end, the firm identifies the ideal qualifications of potential foreign partners. For example, when seeking intermediaries to represent the firm's products in the target market, management might assess and select partners based on criteria such as manufacturing and marketing expertise in the industry, commitment to marketing the product in the target market, and possession of appropriate distribution channels and infrastructure.

The firm should emphasize a good fit between itself and the partner, in terms of common goals and objectives, as well as complementarity of resources and competencies. Managers must be assured of a harmonious partnership in a dynamic environment. Other characteristics that companies consider when seeking foreign partners include

- financial resources and stability, with the ability to invest in the venture and ensure future growth;
- competent managers, technical staff, and sales personnel;
- strong knowledge of the industry and of the market;
- established reputation in the market, with adequate links to the local government;
- ready access to distribution channels and end users; and
- sense of commitment and loyalty to the exporter.

Where the partner is lacking in one or more critical areas, the firm should be prepared to strengthen the partner's capabilities by transferring appropriate know-how or other resources.

Finding the Right Partner

In international markets, screening and evaluating partners pose numerous challenges. The firm should consult various sources and conduct field research in order to identify prospective partners and gather background information. Numerous resources are available for developing lists of partner candidates abroad, including business directories, trade journals, industry magazines, and consulting firms. Online guides such as Kompass and Dun & Bradstreet are very helpful for Europe and the United States, respectively. National governments frequently offer inexpensive services that assist firms in finding partners in specific markets. The knowledge portal globalEDGE™ provides additional resources, including several diagnostic tools, to support making systematic choices about alternative partner candidates.

Field research is vital, particularly in the latter stages of assessing potential partners. Field research is accomplished by conducting onsite visits and gathering research from independent sources and trade shows. It is wise to request prospective partners to prepare a formal business plan before entering an agreement. In doing so, the firm can gauge the resources, capabilities, sophistication, and commitment of the prospective partner.

Activity Six: Estimate Company Sales Potential

Once the firm has devised a short list of promising country markets, verified industry market potential, and identified qualified business partners, the next major activity in GMOA is to estimate company sales potential in each country. Company sales potential is an estimate of the share of annual industry sales that the firm expects to generate in a given target market. Estimating company sales potential can be particularly challenging, as it requires the researcher to obtain fine-grained information from the market. The researcher usually must make fundamental assumptions about the market and project the firm's expenses and revenues for 3–5 years into the future. Given all the potential variables involved, the task is demanding. Successful estimation of company sales potential requires exercising substantial judgment, based on knowledge obtained from the target market.

In estimating company sales potential, managers collect and review research findings with a view to addressing the following key concerns:

- *Risk tolerance of senior managers.* Success in the contemplated market hinges on the level of resources that top management is willing to commit, which in turn depends on the extent of management's tolerance for risk in the market.

- *Financial and human resources.* The quality and quantity of the firm's resources are a major factor in determining the proficiency and speed with which it can enter the market.
- *Pricing and financing of sales.* The extent to which pricing and financing are attractive to both customers and channel members is vital to initial entry and ultimate success in the market.
- *Network in the market.* The extent of the firm's existing relationships with customers, channel members, suppliers, consultants, financial institutions, and facilitators can strongly influence ultimate success of the venture.
- *Partner capabilities.* The resources and competencies of foreign partners help to determine how quickly the firm can enter and generate sales in the market.
- *Access to distribution channels.* The ability to establish and make best use of intermediaries and distribution infrastructure often determines short- and long-term success.
- *Intensity of competition.* Local or third-country competitors may intensify their own selling efforts when confronted by new entrants.
- *Market penetration timetable.* A key decision is whether the firm should opt for gradual or rapid market entry. Gradual entry affords time to refine and leverage appropriate strategies but may cede some advantages to competitors in getting established in the market.

The process of estimating company sales involves examining additional variables, as well as making assumptions in areas where the firm may lack specific knowledge. There is likely to be substantial uncertainty, and many decisions hinge on making skillful judgments. The process of estimating demand is often more of an art than a science. Some managers prepare multiple estimates based on best, worst, and most-likely case scenarios of company success, so that entry can be appropriately judged from various angles. Market success typically depends on factors both controllable by management (such as prices charged to intermediaries and customers) and uncontrollable factors (such as the intensity and reactions of competitors). Table 2.2 illustrates many of the variables to investigate when estimating company sales potential.

Practical Methods for Estimating Company Sales Potential

Managers employ several methods for estimating company sales potential abroad. These are reviewed next.

- *Conducting trade audits.* Using this approach, the researcher visits retail outlets and interviews channel intermediaries to inquire about the potential for product sales in the market. The trade audit also helps to reveal customer characteristics, appropriate pricing levels, and the nature of competitors. By conducting a trade audit, the researcher views market potential from the perspective of intermediaries who often possess deep knowledge of

Table 2.2   Key Variables to Investigate in Opportunity Assessment

VARIABLE	TYPICAL DIMENSIONS
Customer receptivity	• Perceived benefits of the product or service • Nature of marketing communications directed at customer
Brand positioning	• Unique selling proposition of product • Superior features of the product, compared to competitors' offerings
Channel effort and productivity	• Margins and incentives offered to intermediaries
Competitors	• Competitive intensity • Relative strength • Potential reactions to market entrants
Customers	• Size of customer segment • Purchasing power • Demand growth • Demographic characteristics
Pricing	• Cost of product or service "landed" in the foreign market • Usual margins for intermediaries • Basic pricing strategy (e.g., penetration, skimming, life-cycle pricing, cost-based pricing, differentiated pricing)

the marketplace and customers. The audit may also indicate the need for differing approaches to distribution.

- *Obtaining estimates from local partners.* Here the researcher interviews local collaborators—such as suppliers, franchisees, and banks—already experienced in the market. Such entities are often well positioned to advise about sales potential.

- *Surveying end users.* The researcher develops and administers a questionnaire to a sample of customers to determine the likely level of potential sales. Alternatively, the researcher may conduct focus groups with selected representative customers. These methods are described in subsequent chapters.

- *Engaging in test marketing.* Some firms undertake a limited entry in the foreign market to measure sales potential directly and to deepen understanding of the market. This approach helps forecast longer term sales and may be especially appropriate in developing economies and emerging markets where secondary information sources are often very limited.

- *Using analogy.* Here the researcher draws on known statistics from one country to gain insights into the same phenomenon for a similar country. For example, suppose the firm wants to market candy bars in Pakistan. If the researcher knows the total consumption of candy bars in India, then, assuming candy bar consumption does not vary much between Pakistan and India, a rough estimate of Pakistan's consumption can be made, making an adjustment for the difference in population.

- *Using proxy indicators.* This refers to estimating sales of one product by knowing sales of another, similar product. For example, if the researcher wants to estimate sales of computer keyboards but only has historical sales data on computer monitors, it is still possible to achieve a reasonable estimate of keyboard sales, since keyboards and monitors usually go together. The approach is appropriate when two products exhibit a complementary demand relationship.

- *Assessing competitors.* The firm can benchmark itself against a principal competitor(s) in the market and estimate the level of sales it can potentially attract away from the competitor(s).

Note, however, that this approach is potentially risky because competitors may hold very substantial resources or operate in different market segments.

Whatever the rationale for pursuing international opportunities, it is critical to conduct a systematic and comprehensive assessment of each opportunity. In the next chapter, we will delve into the fundamentals of international research and the tools and procedures that firms apply to understand individual foreign markets.

CHAPTER 3

Fundamentals of International Market Research

Managers need objective information and insights in order to make the best decisions for superior performance in international business. For success abroad, as in many of life's endeavors, it is critical to do your homework. Comprehensive data and insights allow managers to fully capitalize on global market opportunities. Differences in economic conditions, legal systems, physical infrastructure, business practices, as well as obstacles of language and culture, mean that international business is fraught with substantial uncertainty and risk. Internationalizing firms conduct market research to identify opportunities and constraints in individual markets; locate and qualify prospective customers, intermediaries, and facilitators; and determine the best ways to operate in foreign markets In addition, research reveals vital information about competitors, providing valuable competitive intelligence, such as the sources and intensity of competition, whether from other foreign firms or from local production.

Key informational needs that arise in the course of conducting international business include the following:

- What are the most attractive country markets?
- What is the degree of suitability of our products and services for target country customers?
- How substantial is the industry market potential in each market?
- What level of company sales can we anticipate?
- What do we know about the customers and their requirements?
- What do we know about distribution channel intermediaries? How qualified are potential distribution partners?

- What is the most appropriate mode of market entry? For example, should we enter via exporting, licensing, or foreign direct investment?
- How competitive is the market? What are the relative strengths and weaknesses of rival firms?
- What government regulations apply to our operations (e.g., regulations related to marketing, selling, pricing, and distribution)?
- What should be the key features of our marketing strategy?

Three Types of Research Methods

Companies undertake various types of international market research projects. For formal or large-scale research projects, it is generally best to prepare a written *research design plan*. The research design summarizes the types of information that the firm is seeking and the type of research that it will conduct. There are three major types of research that firms undertake in international markets: descriptive research, exploratory research, and causal research.

The purpose of *descriptive research* is to provide an accurate description of something that is occurring. For example, descriptive research might be used to describe the nature of a particular category of customers. Firms routinely conduct basic descriptive research using informal means. For example, a marketing manager might ask sales personnel about the nature of consumers that patronize particular stores. However, in order to ensure that findings result in valid marketing decisions, the researcher generally should adhere to the scientific method and follow rigorous research methods. This requires the researcher to possess a solid knowledge of research methods and data analysis.

Exploratory research seeks to discover general information about a topic that is not well understood by the marketer. For example, suppose the marketer has heard that a competitor has developed a product that relies on a new technology. The researcher might undertake exploratory research to learn more about the technology and how customers are using it in the marketplace. Alternatively, suppose the firm is considering doing business in Russia but is concerned about reports that product counterfeiting is a problem there. In this case, the researcher might delve into articles and other information via the Internet to learn about the rate of counterfeiting and the nature of intellectual property laws and enforcements in Russia.

When undertaking *causal research*, the marketer manipulates one variable, called the "independent variable," and then studies its affect on another variable, called the "dependent variable." In essence, the marketer is conducting an experiment. For example, suppose the marketer wants to find out how various price levels affect consumer purchases of the firm's product. In this case, the marketer might charge 20 euros for the product in Frankfurt and 25 euros for the same product in Munich. Assuming that consumers in these German cities are very similar, the marketer would be able to determine the effect of these different prices on sales. The marketer also would likely formulate a "hypothesis" that the cheaper price will result in, or "cause," higher sales volume in Frankfurt and that the higher price will result in lower sales volume in Munich.

Causal research can be used to test other phenomena as well, such as what might happen to sales if changes are made to a product's design or if advertising is changed. If performed well, causal research can be used for forecasting what might happen if the changes are made. However, to be effective, causal research must be designed well and carefully controlled to ensure that other factors do not affect the dependent variable.

The Knowledge Pyramid

Market research should aim to generate three major types of input: data, information and intelligence and knowledge and insights. Together, these inputs make up the knowledge pyramid shown in Figure 3.1.

- *Data* refer to raw facts, figures, and observations that have not been organized or arranged.
- *Information and intelligence* refer to facts, figures, and observations that have been organized or arranged around a specific theme.
- *Knowledge and insights* refer to information and intelligence that have been processed, analyzed, and interpreted, and can lead to action.

As Figure 3.1 shows, each knowledge input builds on the preceding level. That is, data are first acquired, then processed into information and intelligence, and finally translated and absorbed as knowledge and insights by managers.

Let's illustrate the differences among the three types of knowledge inputs. Table 3.1 provides specific examples on how simple international business data can be transformed into information and intelligence, and then converted into knowledge and insights.

For example, national trade statistics, such as a nation's exports and imports with other countries, by themselves are useful and interesting. The researcher can do a simple statistical analysis and identify key trends in exports and imports. However, the researcher can gain even more useful insights when such data are arranged by each trading partner. For example, if we examine Singapore's trade with other countries, we find that much of it is with its neighbors in the South Asian region. Similarly, Hong Kong's major trading partner is China. This insight has useful implications for Western firms. These companies may choose to use Singapore as a gateway or their hub for Southeast Asia, and they might choose Hong Kong as their gateway to China.

Globalization and technological advances facilitate cost-effective acquisition of data and information, while increasing the efficiency with

Figure 3.1
The knowledge pyramid

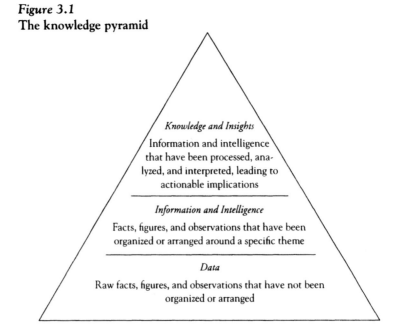

Knowledge and Insights
Information and intelligence
that have been processed, analyzed, and interpreted, leading to
actionable implications

Information and Intelligence
Facts, figures, and observations that have been
organized or arranged around a specific theme

Data
Raw facts, figures, and observations that have not been
organized or arranged

Table 3.1   Examples of How the Knowledge Pyramid Works

DATA	INFORMATION AND INTELLIGENCE	KNOWLEDGE AND INSIGHTS
National trade statistics	Arranged by a country's imports and exports to nearby countries	Implications about the pattern of trade-flows among countries, including the finding that some countries serve as gateways to others
Worker wages	Arranged by components of total compensation: basic pay, bonuses, fringe benefits, and incentives	Implications about the costs of rewarding and motivating employees; finding that basic pay makes up only a small percentage of total compensation in developing economies
Population	Arranged by age, region, and density (e.g., urban versus rural)	Insights about the size of a market; implications about concentration of customers; insights about what cities and regions to target in order to maximize the effectiveness of marketing activities
Income	Arranged by purchasing power parity, disposable income, distribution of income, and household income	Implications regarding the purchasing capacity of consumers; insights about how to target a specific market segment; knowledge that leads to the most appropriate pricing strategies
Retail outlets	Arranged by size, location, and average turnover	Implications regarding the most appropriate locations of retail outlets; insights that aid in capacity planning; knowledge about how best to set up logistical arrangements
Government regulations	Arranged by business policy area, degree of intensity, degree of enforcement, and cost of implementation	Implications about ranking of countries based on intensity of regulations; implications about whether or not the firm should enter the market and what market entry mode to use
Media habits	Arranged by media types, frequency of viewership, frequency of readership, and cost per exposure	Implications about ideal choices of communications media and relative spending

which managers transform that data and information into intelligence and knowledge. In the contemporary "knowledge society," any organization that deals with complex and changing international environments needs to process information efficiently and create new knowledge. For example, a bank entering Europe would benefit from the knowledge that annual customer fees for banking services vary widely, ranging from 31 euros in the Netherlands to 501 euros in Italy (Ng, 2004).

Figure 3.2 provides an organizational framework on the informational needs of international managers. As the figure suggests, while all businesses have accumulated some knowledge of domestic business activity, they need to add substantial new knowledge to this base with respect to cross-border transactions, country and regional knowledge, and cross-cultural knowledge. The figure includes examples of the specific types of expertise that make up these knowledge bases.

In order to address the research questions that confront the firm, the researcher must gather data from various sources. When gathering data, the researcher generally has two choices: acquire preexisting data *or* undertake new research. The first option is associated with *secondary data*—preexisting facts, figures, and observations that have been gathered and made available for consumption by others. The second option is associated

Figure 3.2
The four layers of knowledge in international business

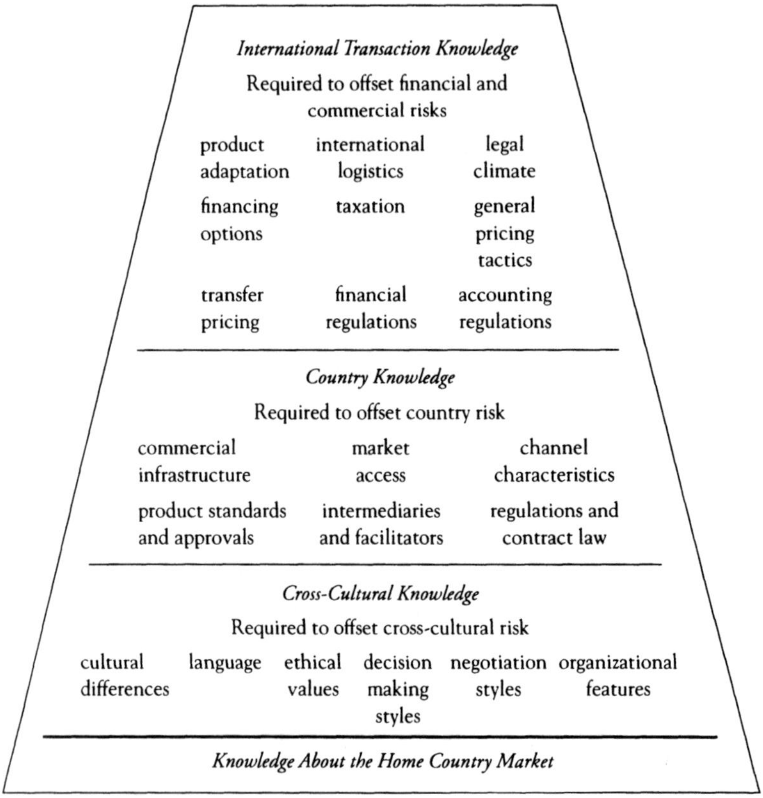

International Transaction Knowledge
Required to offset financial and commercial risks

product adaptation	international logistics	legal climate
financing options	taxation	general pricing tactics
transfer pricing	financial regulations	accounting regulations

Country Knowledge
Required to offset country risk

| commercial infrastructure | market access | channel characteristics |
| product standards and approvals | intermediaries and facilitators | regulations and contract law |

Cross-Cultural Knowledge
Required to offset cross-cultural risk

cultural differences   language   ethical values   decision making styles   negotiation styles   organizational features

Knowledge About the Home Country Market

with obtaining *primary data*—original data that the researcher gathers via a customized research effort, with the aim of addressing the specific problem at hand.

Both types of data serve the researcher well and typically provide complementary insights. Initially, researchers collect secondary data because it can be obtained cheaply and quickly. Sources for secondary data include government agencies, industry trade associations, company-provided information, annual reports, press releases, white papers, presentations, news and media outlets, and competitors' Web sites and newsletters. Most secondary data is obtained in libraries and via the Internet. Research to collect secondary data is often called "desk research" because it is accomplished while seated at a desk at the office or a library as opposed to field research. The main shortcoming of secondary data, however, is that it usually cannot answer all of the firm's research questions.

For example, the Swedish company IKEA is the world's largest furniture retailer. IKEA has been expanding into foreign markets, such as Turkey. IKEA managers conduct market research to understand how best to succeed in each market. IKEA researchers uncover considerable information from secondary data sources about the profile of furniture buyers in Turkey. But deeper insights into the nature of Turkish furniture consumers can be gained only by collecting primary data.

Usually the approach is to use secondary data to answer as many of the research questions as possible. Then, when research questions remain that cannot be answered using secondary data, the firm resorts to collecting primary data. Research that seeks to obtain primary data is often called "field research" because the researcher goes into actual business or consumer settings to observe or interact with people to gather information and insights. Primary data are custom-produced data or information that emerge from an original research project. Typically, primary data are collected using surveys, observation, experiments, or focus group interviews. People who fill out surveys are known as "respondents." Survey respondents can be suppliers, customers, channel intermediaries, facilitators, industry experts, and even regulatory agencies. Focus group interviews typically involve open discussions with 5–8 people relevant to the question under study. Gathering primary data is the focus of Chapter 4. In this chapter, we will discuss collecting secondary data.

Obtaining Secondary Data via Desk Research

As indicated earlier, secondary data may be accessible from many sources, including libraries, government agencies, and trade magazines. While much secondary data are available to users freely, some can be secured only by purchasing or subscribing to an information service. Many market research companies charge a fee to users for making various types of secondary data available.

Secondary data can be fairly specific. For example, the U.S. government regularly reports on best market prospects in the aerospace industry. Secondary data sources in the U.S. government might report that Japan's defense agency is seeking to develop a new type of maritime patrol and transport aircraft and that companies in Japan are increasing their purchases of small corporate jets. In Thailand, the construction of a new major airport might suggest substantial demand in Thailand for airport security equipment and baggage handling systems. As these examples reveal, secondary data can help managers to focus on promising international business opportunities.

An important advantage of secondary data is its cost effectiveness. Thus, secondary data are particularly appealing to small firms and other resource-poor companies. Managers new to international business are often pleasantly surprised at the amount and variety of information available from secondary data sources. In addition to libraries and online portals such as globalEDGE™ (www.globaledge.msu.edu), there are various other data sources, at home and abroad. Available information typically ranges from simple trade statistics to in-depth market surveys.

Managers can consult statistics on their home country's share of a foreign market for the purpose of gauging the overall competitiveness of home country producers. By examining statistics over a period of time, the researcher can ascertain which markets are growing and which are shrinking. Market surveys provide a narrative description and assessment of particular markets along with relevant statistics. They are frequently based on original, in-country research, often by commercial staff at embassies abroad, and may include specific information on both buyers and competitors.

Limitations of Secondary Data

Although secondary data are easy to access and cost-effective, they also have significant limitations:

1. Desired information may be *unavailable* or out-of-date.
2. Data may be too *broad-based*—that is, not specific enough to adequately address the firm's research questions.
3. The *units* in which the data are presented may not be meaningful.
4. The source of the data may not provide sufficient supporting material to allow the researcher to judge the *quality* of the research.
5. The data sources may lack *reliability and credibility*. Some secondary data may simply be inaccurate.

For example, although Vietnam is said to have a per capita gross domestic product (GDP) of about $3,000 per year, the figure may be inaccurate because a substantial informal or unrecorded economy exists in Vietnam that is not included in official government statistics. Smuggling across the Cambodian-Vietnam border is said to exceed official trade between the two countries. Much of Vietnam's international trade is based on countertrade, which is often difficult to assess (Storey & Robinson, 2004). Thus, national and per capita income in Vietnam are difficult to calculate. Accordingly, it is best for the researcher to consult a variety of alternative sources of secondary data and then cross-check them in order to ensure findings are valid and accurate.

The Internet as a Resource for Secondary Data

The Internet is used widely for accessing secondary data. There are thousands of sites that facilitate data collection on markets, prospective customers, and competitors. Managers can access data on industry and aggregate global marketing transactions, individual reports on foreign firms, and information on relevant laws and regulations at home and abroad. Examples of reports available online include news accounts, statistics, regulatory information, research reports, reference books, "how to" guides, videos, opinions, and discussion forums. Managers can join online communities that focus on globalization issues and international business. While online resources have their own limitations, the Internet is extremely cost-effective for collecting secondary data.

One of the most effective uses of the Internet is as a source for collecting detailed competitive intelligence. Researchers can review competitors' Web sites, which reveal information about the products or projects, advertising strategies, potential alliances, financial performance, and news accounts of current or potential rivals.

Some news services incorporate "push" technology that delivers a continuous stream of information updates and late-breaking news stories automatically to users' e-mail addresses. Such services help managers to stay abreast of the latest developments of competing firms. Although not a substitute for in-depth background research, push technology keeps managers up-to-date within specific search parameters. Other business intelligence providers offer customized reports on industries and individual companies. As with all forms of secondary data, researchers should cross-check information obtained from online sources with other sources.

The two greatest advantages of online research are its low cost and high speed, which are particularly relevant for research done internationally where customers may be located all over the world. The Internet provides an efficient way to tap into buyer opinions, via focus groups and large-scale surveys. A key disadvantage for international research, however, is that the Internet is not widely available in many countries. Moreover, most Internet users tend to be well educated, affluent, and young. Thus, they are not strongly representative of many international customers, especially those located in developing economies and emerging markets. Appendix A provides a listing of popular Internet sites for obtaining secondary data on international business.

GlobalEDGE™ Knowledge Portal

Researchers can avoid potentially inaccurate or outdated online data by consulting a credible knowledge portal such as globalEDGE™. This portal connects to a wealth of credible, accurate, up-to-date, and easy-to-access data, information, insights, and learning resources on business activities on a global and regional scale. GlobalEDGE™ includes country-level data and information with maps, key statistics, history, economy, government, and links to country-specific resources, stock markets, and recent events. It is a gateway to specialized knowledge on countries, cross-border business transactions, and international transactions of various types.

Other Online Resources

In addition to globalEDGE™, the researcher can consult dozens of other reliable knowledge portals. A good starting point for learning about individual countries is the portal of the U.S. Central Intelligence Agency (CIA), the *CIA World Factbook* (http://www.cia.gov/cia/publications/factbook/). Additional sources include the U.S. Department of Commerce export portal (http://export.gov/); the *Statistical Yearbook of the United Nations*; and publications of the World Bank, such as *World Development Indicators*. The World Bank also offers an excellent database covering national business regulations and their enforcement for 155 countries (http://www.doingbusiness.org/). The Organization for Economic Cooperation and Development (OECD) also publishes various useful publications. Statistical abstracts and annual almanacs for each country of interest are also available. For example, the *Asahi Shinbun* (a Japanese newspaper) publishes the *Japan Almanac* each year for Japan. Conveniently for the user, globalEDGE™ provides an excellent gateway to all of these resources and more.

A particularly useful resource for international business research is the National Trade Data Bank (NTDB), provided by the U.S. Department of Commerce. It is accessible both online (www.stat-usa.gov) and via CD-ROM, which are both updated monthly and available by subscription. The NTDB is a comprehensive database of the most up-to-date international trade, investment, and economic information, presented in a convenient format. It contains trade leads, resources, and highly specific information on conditions and business practices for markets around the world. Of particular interest are market and country research reports including "Country Commercial Guides," "Best Market Reports," and "Industry Sector Analysis Reports." Trade associations such as world trade clubs and domestic and international chambers of commerce also provide a wealth of information on various topics. In the next chapter, we will provide a detailed explanation of primary data.

Food for Thought: Dimensions of International Consumer Behavior

When it comes to marketing consumer products in international markets, the researcher often wants to develop a thorough understanding of the *psychological profiles* and *sociological identities* of the consumers who make up target markets. In order to understand the psychological profiles of potential customers, the researcher investigates consumer motives, perceptions, personalities, attitudes, beliefs, and values, and attempts to link these to consumer purchase intentions. To measure the impact of their sociological identities on purchase behavior, the researcher investigates buyers' cultural values, traditions, and ethnicity, and attempts to link these to the development of consumers' specific needs and tastes. Other variables of interest include the reference groups with whom consumers associate, social class standing, and societal norms. We will now explore some of these issues as they relate to international market research.

The Psychological Ingredients of Purchase Behavior: The Case of Consumer Products

In the international marketing of consumer products, one of the most important determinants of buying behavior and purchase intentions is the motive of the consumer. Motives are generally based on the aspirational aspects of a person's self-concept. Motives help the consumer to establish her identity—that is, what she means to herself and to others around her. Aspirations, expressions of the consumer's self-concept, are culturally bounded. Some cultures thrive on pursuing positive, performance-oriented aspirational goals; other cultures have very utilitarian goals; still others are sensitive to peer groups and seek to conform to the norms of the society in which they live (Arnould et al., 2002, pp. 378–379; Markus & Kitayama, 1991).

A second ingredient in motivation is involvement, which refers to the extent to which the consumer is excited, engaged, or passionate about achieving a certain consumption goal (Arnould et al., 2002, p. 379). In some countries, for example, consumers seek high levels of social status. Consumers in status-oriented cultures are driven to accumulate material goods and engage passionately in purchasing goods and services that reflect their perception of socially accepted norms. In other cultures, achieving societal status is of lesser importance. It is important for the marketer to determine the principal motives that drive purchase behavior in each market. Such understanding assists with formulating decisions about what products to offer, and the extent to which each offering can be standardized, or whether it should be customized to suit individual needs in target markets.

Perceptions help consumers interpret the world around them and assign meaning to that world (Arnould et al., 2002). Consumers make a purchase based on their perceptions of the attributes of the marketer's product. Attributes can be concrete (price, warranty) or abstract (quality, value). How consumers perceive these attributes varies across markets because of differing cultural backgrounds. Similarities and differences in perceptions about product quality, value for money spent, warranty, and price help the marketer to determine to what extent marketing strategy can be standardized and to what extent marketing must be adapted to suit individual needs. For example, toothpaste may be perceived as a cavity reducer in one market and a tooth-whitening agent in another. In one market consumers may perceive shampoo as an essential ingredient in hair care while in another it may be perceived as unnecessary, and hand soap may be used to wash one's hair.

Personality refers to the distinctive and enduring patterns of thoughts, emotions, and behaviors that describe how the individual responds to stimuli in his environment (Arnould et al., 2002, p. 254). Marketers are primarily concerned about delivering a superior value proposition to target consumers. Personality can aid in identifying appropriate target segments and designing the most appropriate marketing strategies. One type of personality trait is "consumer ethnocentrism"—the proclivity to view one's own group as the center of the universe, to interpret other social units from the perspective of one's own group, and to reject persons or products that are culturally dissimilar while blindly accepting those that are culturally similar (Shimp & Sharma, 1987). Consumer ethnocentrism is a major factor affecting purchase behavior in markets worldwide (Sharma, Shimp, & Shin, 1995; Steenkamp, ter Hofstede, & Wedel, 1999).

Beliefs are formed on the basis of direct observation or information received from outside sources or by way of inference processes. The consumer learns or forms beliefs about an object and associates that object with a number of attributes. In this manner, the consumer forms beliefs about himself, about other people, about institutions around him, and about products—that is, he makes attributions and becomes disposed toward product purchase (Fishbein & Ajzen, 1975, chap. 1).

The totality of the consumer's beliefs serves as the informational base that determines consumer attitudes—that is, the enduring evaluations of a concept or object, such as a brand, and intentions to purchase that brand. Consumers' attitudes toward a purchase are based on salient beliefs about the brand. Attitudes are enduring and difficult to change. Attitudes lead to attributions that the consumer makes about the brand's attributes and her evaluation of those attributes as positive or negative (Arnould et al., 2002, p. 460).

Attitudes influence purchase behavior in a least four major ways (Arnould et al., 2002, pp. 460–461). The consumer with a utilitarian orientation is driven to consume products that fulfill very practical needs. For example, oral hygiene has high utility in some cultures; consumers in these cultures brush frequently and use various products to achieve superior oral hygiene, including toothpaste, mouth-rinsing liquids, and mouth-cleaning gels. In contrast, in other markets, oral hygiene is not highly valued; consumers in these markets use these products less frequently.

The value-expressive orientation is based on the assumption that the consumer seeks to reflect her self-concept to the world via the brands that she consumes. For example, Japan is a brand-conscious society in which consumers are interested in buying popular brand-name goods. The marketer must account for the value-expressive orientation in order to succeed in these markets.

The ego-defensive orientation is based on the assumption that the consumer aims to protect himself from threats to his ego. While in Western markets such products as mouthwash and underarm sprays find an enthusiastic audience, in other markets these traits are less relevant.

Finally, knowledge orientation addresses the consumer's need for consistency. Western cultures are more inclined toward order and linear thinking in their thoughts about a product. In other cultures, such as those in Asia, people are more comfortable with circular thinking and do not expect a product to necessarily solve a particular problem for them.

The above categories are not mutually exclusive, and two or more orientations may dominate a purchase decision simultaneously. The marketer should seek to understand which are the dominant functions in each country and design marketing strategies accordingly (Arnould et al., 2002, p. 462).

In the final analysis, attitudes predispose the consumer to a set of intentions that indicate a degree of affect (feelings) toward the product, blended with rational evaluations of it. These intentions lead to a specific behavior, such as purchase of the product and postpurchase evaluation. Motives, perceptions, personality, and beliefs lead to the formation of attitudes, which lead to intentions to purchase, which finally lead to purchase and postpurchase behavior (Fishbein & Ajzen, 1975, chap. 1). Measuring each of these and their individual and collective impacts on purchase behavior in multiple markets are significant but challenging tasks that the international marketer should perform in developing strategy and tactics for specific international markets.

The Sociological Ingredients of Purchase Behavior

Perhaps the most significant sociological driver of a consumer's purchase decision is her value system. Values are fundamental to the consumer's evaluations and perceptions of her environment, the context in which she survives. Values are enduring beliefs that a specific mode of conduct is personally or socially preferable to some other mode of conduct. Accordingly, values serve as guiding principles of the consumer's everyday life (Rokeach, 1973; Kahle, 1983). These influences carry the consumer toward purchasing certain products over others—for example, toward purchasing a domestic-versus a foreign-made product, or even choosing between two foreign-made brands, such as a Volkswagen Jetta or a Toyota Camry.

Values exist in an organized value system. Some values are regarded as terminal values, reflecting desired end-states that guide behavior across many different situations. Instrumental values are those needed to achieve these desired end-states. Family security, happiness, salvation, and a sense of belonging are examples of terminal values. Being ambitious, capable, forgiving, honest, imaginative, and loving are examples of instrumental values. Domain-specific values are those that are relevant within a given sphere of activity, such as spirituality (Rokeach, 1973).

Many studies show that values and value systems influence consumption behavior. Through research, marketers can profile a market's value system, segment their markets through the use of value system segmentation (Kamakura & Novak, 1992), and compare markets based on these value systems to determine how best to develop marketing strategies and tactics. Marketers can also measure lifestyles—consumers' activities, interests, and opinions that reflect their values—to gain additional insight into consumption patterns in a market. In marketing, lifestyles are assumed to be the cognitive link between values and behavioral intentions, such as purchasing one brand over other brands. A consumption-related lifestyle defines a system of cognitive associations that relate a set of products or brands to a set of values. Marketers typically use psychographic techniques that involve all of these factors to predict consumer behavior patterns in, and across, markets (Arnould et al., 2002, pp. 270–307).

Value systems can be divided into personal and collective (or societal) values. Personal values are important in consumer decision-making processes and provide indications of consumer's motivations, perceptions, needs, and attitudes. Collective values are also important in that they reflect a society's values, history, and ethnic and geographic heritage. In international business, both personal and collective value systems provide the manager with a useful base for developing effective marketing strategy. Thus, it is important to delve into the consumer's value system via market research efforts (Arnould et al., 2002, chap. 5).

Value system measurement can be accomplished through a variety of metrics developed by scholars and marketing managers during the past several decades. Among the most popular and empirically validated research instruments are Rokeach's Value Survey (RVS; Rokeach, 1973), the VALS system (Mitchell, 1983), the List of Values (Kahle, 1983), Schwartz and Bilsky's Value System (1987, 1990), Hofstede's cultural clusters (1980, 2001), Inglehart's societal value system (1997), and the

GLOBE study of value systems in 62 countries around the world (House, Hanges, Javidan, Dorfman, & Gupta, 2004).

An interesting by-product of value system research is the "means-end" or "laddering" approach built on the assumption that a consumer's purchase behavior can be explained by linking his evaluation of a product's (or brand's) attributes to functional or psychosocial consequences, and ultimately to the satisfaction of his instrumental and terminal values (Gutman, 1982, 1984; Reynolds & Gutman, 1988). Based on the literature on values (mentioned earlier), the laddering approach assumes that when making a purchase decision, consumers evaluate the product's concrete (directly observable characteristics of the product; e.g., price) and abstract (subjective, not directly observable features of the product; e.g., quality) attributes, and link these to functional (tangible results of the product; e.g., "handles well on the road") and psychosocial (psychological or sociological results of product use; e.g., "others will see me as special when I purchase this product") consequences of purchasing that product. They then link these to instrumental (preferred modes of conduct, abstract consequences of product use; e.g., "I will be the center of attention") and terminal (preferred end-states of being; e.g., "I will enhance my self-esteem") values. The application of this approach in international business is particularly interesting since the ladders constructed by consumers in purchasing a product are likely to vary from one national market to another, and do so even within a national market based on regional, demographic, or psychographic (lifestyle) differences.

The marketer may find variations of constructed ladders not only among the Indian and the Chinese markets, for example, but also between the Bengali and the Gujurati Indian communities, or urban versus rural dwellers in India. She may also find that Indian and Chinese urban dwellers are, in fact, more similar to one another than their national rural counterparts. This may lead her to standardize certain elements of strategy across country markets, while custom tailoring other elements for specific country (or segment) markets. The international business literature is replete with applications of this technique to the marketing of fast-moving consumer-goods products.

One of the significant questions international business researchers ask is what really drives consumer behavior in the markets in which they seek to do business (Day & Montgomery, 1999). In this context, Roper Starch Worldwide's (2000) study of nationality, lifestyles, and values shows that even with increased globalization of markets and consumers, nationality remains a dominant driver. Life stages, which compose many demographic measures, are dominant in health-related concerns, media usage, and certain leisure activities. Values help bridge the gap in understanding the similarities and differences beyond nationality and life stages among markets. Indeed, Roper Starch Worldwide's research (2000), which involved 30,000 respondents around the globe, showed that protecting one's family, honesty, health and fitness, self-esteem, self-reliance, justice, freedom, friendship, knowledge, and learning are the top 10 shared values among these consumers.

However, some regional variations were also found. For example, in North America, individuality, romance, excitement, adventure, and social tolerance were at a higher level, while in Latin America, romance, sex, spirituality, traditional gender roles, and faith were relatively more important. Some values showed polarizing variations from one culture to the next. For example, faith was the highest rated value in Indonesia, Egypt, and Saudi Arabia, whereas it was 45th in France. Self-reliance was 3rd and 4th in Mexico and Russia, respectively, but it was 33rd in Saudi Arabia. Romance was 9th in Thailand but 56th in India.

Based on this research, Roper Starch Worldwide (2000) developed six "universal" market segments based on consumers' groupings around certain sets of values: (a) creatives (renaissance people who are deeply involved in all areas of life); (b) fun seekers (party people who stress social and hedonistic pursuits); (c) intimates (people who value relationships above all else); (d) strivers (workaholics driven by a desire for status and wealth); (e) devouts (traditionalists who have strong convictions about faith, modesty, duty, and past); and (f) altruists (humanitarians who place higher priority on social values and the world at large). Roper Starch Worldwide (2000) also found that many of these categories intersect. For example, the "influential Americans" group in this classification includes 15% creatives, 10% altruists, 8% devouts, 5% intimates, 4% funseekers, and 2% strivers (Roper Starch Worldwide, 2000).

Value transformations are most likely a function of the level of education and "worldliness" in a given market. According to Roper Starch Worldwide

(2000), as advanced education reaches more and more of the global population, certain values will naturally grow or decline. Self-esteem, self-reliance, stable relationships, knowledge, learning, wisdom, enduring love, and freedom will likely increase as education rises, while values such as faith and respecting elders will likely decrease. Generational differences in values that are present today will likely continue into the future as well. For example, while family security and honesty will probably remain the top two values across all age groups throughout the world, continuing today's trend into the near future, third-ranked values are likely to evolve. Health and fitness (the current first-ranked value for today's teenager group) might give way to security as this cohort emerges into adulthood, and this may, in turn, give way to self-esteem as the cohort moves to its thirty-something years (Roper Starch Worldwide, 2000). In marketing, it is necessary but insufficient to develop a deep understanding of consumers' values.

In summary, sociological drivers of consumer behavior, such as consumer value systems, act as foretellers of consumer purchase patterns. Consumers' values are structured into hierarchies ranging from the most to the least centrally held and reflect the desirable end-states that transcend specific situations and lead to desired behaviors. Through socialization and cognitive development, individuals in all societies learn to represent their value systems as conscious goals, use culturally shared symbols and language to communicate these values to each other, and attach attributions to them (Arnould et al., 2002, pp. 285–290). These are reflected in consumers' purchase behavior, are significant in segmentation, targeting, and positioning considerations and are key in the shaping of marketing mix decisions (Wedel & Kamakura, 2000). They are particularly important in international business as we find both similarities and differences in the value profiles of the markets in which the firm operates and can use these in designing strategies to fulfill consumer needs and desires in these markets.

CHAPTER 4

Customized Research Using Primary Data

As the search for knowledge and information progresses, the researcher eventually begins to ask highly specific research questions that cannot be addressed using secondary data. At this stage, the researcher should seek primary data. Here, research evolves from addressing general questions, such as "What markets should we target with our product?" to specific questions, such as "What are the specific habits of consumers who are likely to buy and use our product?" Secondary data are insufficient to answer specialized questions, and thus the firm begins to collect primary data. At this stage, the researcher initiates a customized, original research effort that seeks answers from designated respondents. This involves collecting unique data that no one has collected before.

Overview of Primary Research Methods

Research to obtain primary data is typically conducted directly in the target market through observation, surveys, or focus group interviews. Field research such as this provides information on very specific issues related to the nature of customer demand; market segments; and the best approaches for designing and launching the product or service, as well as its pricing, promotion, and distribution. In this way, primary data is typically collected in the latter stages of market entry planning when the firm already has a good idea of what products it intends to sell abroad, the particular countries where it intends to sell them, and other general research questions that have already been answered using secondary data.

For example, cultural values affect buying behavior but are abstract and usually assessed as part of field research. In China, foreign companies enhance brand recognition by appealing to consumers' self-actualization needs. Over 300 million people in more than 100 Chinese cities now earn an income that can afford most discretionary consumer goods. As part of their field research, some companies have discovered that Chinese consumers favor brands that emphasize specific values, including "well-being," "harmony," "tradition," and "belonging." Marketers across the board from Unilever to Volkswagen embed these and other Chinese values in the development of brands targeted to China, creating strong value propositions for customers (Lee & Hall, 2004). Knowledge on such issues can be acquired only via field research to collect primary data.

Customized market research has the advantage of being tailored to the firm's particular needs, providing specific answers to specific questions. More complex or costly international projects require collecting more primary data. The number and variety of research questions can seem limitless, and the cost of large-scale field research can run to hundreds of thousands of dollars. Thus, the cost of collecting primary data should be balanced against the cost of making potentially expensive blunders that result from uninformed decision making.

An example of what can be accomplished with primary data is the South Korean firm Samsung. In the 1990s Samsung had a reputation for low-quality products. By 2004 Samsung had become number one in worldwide sales of TV sets, video recorders, flat-panel screens, computer monitors, and PC memory, with a reputation for style, luxury, and design—often surpassing Japanese rival Sony. Samsung's success was achieved via innovation and research and development (R&D) driven by extensive customer research. Samsung spent tens of millions of dollars on field research to find out what consumers really desire ("As good," 2005).

Methods for Collecting Primary Data

Securing primary data entails using one or more of several research methods. These include observation, experiments, surveys, focus groups, trade fairs, and trade missions. We will now turn to a discussion of these methods.

Observation and Experiments

Observation is a method for collecting primary data in which the researcher directly observes and records the behavior, actions, and facts in a situation of interest. Observation aims at understanding what customers do, rather than why they do it. For example, the toy manufacturer Fisher-Price might invite a group of local preschoolers to its offices in Brazil and allow them to play in a room containing a variety of their toy products. The children are then observed to see which toys Brazilian children seem to prefer. Microsoft might send researchers into software stores in Germany to ascertain the typical prices charged for various competing brands of spreadsheet software. The food manufacturer Morinaga employs scanner technology at supermarkets to better understand consumer purchasing patterns of its products. Researchers, however, cannot observe feelings, attitudes, and private behaviors. For this reason, observations are often combined with other research techniques.

Another method for collecting primary data is through experiments. Here the researcher manipulates one or more independent variables (e.g., advertising or price) and observes how a dependent variable (e.g., sales volume) changes in response to these manipulations. Experiments attempt to establish "cause-and-effect" relationships and are commonly used in test marketing. For example, soft-drink producers such as Coca-Cola conduct controlled taste tests in foreign markets to see how local consumers respond to various formulations of the soft drink. Here, differences in beverage taste are the independent variables, and expressed consumer preference is the dependent variable. Alternatively, researchers at Hewlett-Packard might try to figure out the best promotional method for selling its calculators in China by conducting extensive newspaper advertising in Shanghai, but they run *no* newspaper advertising in Beijing. They then note changes in sales volume at the firm's sales outlets in each city. A key disadvantage of experiments is that they are difficult to implement in foreign countries, due to differences in language, culture, and other factors. Consequently, experimentation is seldom used for international research.

Survey Research

A widely used research method is the survey, which involves gathering primary data from respondents by mail, telephone, personal interviews, or online. Typically, a questionnaire is created and then respondents are asked to express their thoughts and opinions. The consumers or managers to whom a survey is directed are known as "subjects," and those who actually respond to the survey are called "respondents." Subjects respond by completing a questionnaire or other research instrument. A questionnaire is a collection of questions that aim to measure a set of variables and "constructs" (complex concepts composed of two or more variables). Surveys are the most popular method for collecting primary data in international research.

However, surveys encounter various challenges because of differences in language, culture, and economic characteristics of target subjects. Reaching subjects is often slow or cumbersome. Most people in developing countries, for example, lack immediate access to telephones or the Internet. Mail delivery may be compromised due to inadequate postal systems or inaccurate mailing addresses. In Venezuela, houses often have individual names instead of numbers. In Japan, street addresses are usually assigned in order of when the houses were built and, therefore, do not follow a chronological sequence.

Philips, the electronics company based in the Netherlands, makes various products including electric shavers, coffee makers, car phones, and flat screen televisions. Recent research revealed that U.S. consumers did not recognize the Philips name. Seeking to establish itself as a global brand, Philips launched a survey study in which 14,000 people were interviewed in 17 countries about their knowledge of and preferences for Philips products. Findings revealed five cross-national market segments, such as the "dream seekers" who view buying expensive electronics as the attainment of a dream. Another segment was aware of the Philips brand name but was fearful of technology. Philips used the study results to develop a global advertising campaign to appeal to the various market segments. In the United States, 4 months after launching the campaign, Philips' brand recognition jumped nearly 44%. The campaign met its global objectives as well. International research based on primary data collection was critical to this success (Edy, 1999).

Pros and Cons of Survey Research Methods

Each of the survey research methods used in collecting primary data has advantages and disadvantages. The issue of which contact method to use involves a trade-off between the speed and cost of information collection and the accuracy of the information.

Mail-based contact is best for reaching a widely dispersed sample, avoiding bias problems, ensuring respondent anonymity, and minimizing costs. In some countries, however, mail surveys may not be effective because of unreliable postal systems.

The Internet is a relatively new innovation in gathering primary data. It provides a quick and cost-effective way to tap into buyer opinions, through focus groups and large-scale surveys. Online surveys are best for employing visual aids, reaching a very large sample, assuring respondent anonymity, obtaining data relatively quickly, and minimizing the cost of data collection.

Telephone interviews allow for interaction, flexibility in the interview process, widely dispersed samples, rapid data collection, and cost-effectiveness.

Personal interviews enjoy most of the same advantages of telephone interviews, with the added advantages of allowing the use of visual aids, and the ability to ask in-depth questions and to observe respondent reactions more closely. However, personal interviews are usually the most costly of data collection methods.

Focus Group Studies

A focus group is a method of collecting primary data in which a trained moderator facilitates discussion with a group of subjects on a specific topic. Focus groups facilitate rapid collection of large amounts of information and provide detailed information or reveal hidden issues that would not necessarily emerge in individual interviews. However, because the meeting does not usually involve more than a dozen individuals, findings often cannot be generalized to the population of interest. Moreover, peer pressure or other group phenomena may lead to biased or invalid responses.

Participation in International Trade Fairs and Trade Missions

Attending an industry-specific international trade fair (also known as a trade show) in the target country or region is a very effective method for collecting market data. Annual trade fairs are large-scale gatherings at which numerous companies in the same industry exhibit their products. They are held at a public location and attended by buyers, suppliers, distributors, and other interested parties. For example, the International Jewelry Show is held each year in Hong Kong. Italy sponsors an annual event to promote pollution-control equipment. The International Franchise Fair is held each year in Mexico for firms interested in entering Mexico via franchising, such as fast-food restaurants and auto rental agencies. Malaysia holds an annual fair to promote education and training services. There are many hundreds of such events held each year around the world.

Trade fairs are an economical way to quickly learn about potential customers, competitors, and longer term trends in the market of interest. Trade fairs provide a great opportunity to meet prospective intermediaries and test the sales potential of a product or product line. Trade fairs can represent a region within a country, all of the country, or a broad region, such as Northern Europe. Trade fairs are sponsored either by governments or private organizations. In the United States, the Department of Commerce sponsors numerous trade fairs abroad and is also an excellent resource for finding fairs offered around the world. More generally, information on trade fairs, including locations, dates, and categories, can be obtained via the Internet or from government sources that specialize in international trade.

Once the firm has decided to target a specific country, participation in an international trade mission is helpful for directly contacting potential buyers, distributors, and other useful parties in the target country. A trade mission is an organized visit of businesspeople to a foreign market by a sponsoring organization for the purpose of meeting potential customers, intermediaries, and government officials. Trade missions are usually organized by trade associations or by state, provincial, or federal governments. The organizer handles all of the travel and lodging arrangements, as well as meetings with key contacts in the destination country. For example, the U.S. Department of Commerce sponsored a business development trade mission to Afghanistan, an oil equipment and services mission to Vietnam and Singapore, and a health care technologies mission to several countries in Europe. The department's Web site (www.trade .gov) describes upcoming trade missions.

Trade missions are often organized around a trade fair so participants can accomplish a great deal in only one trip abroad. Trade missions exist because a group generally has more power and can achieve much more than individual firms operating alone. Participants make useful contacts in government, industry, and key areas abroad. A trade mission can also be an inexpensive way to travel to target markets because of economies-of-scale in travel and because sponsoring governments may subsidize all or part of the trip. Important government officials who lead trade missions can be especially helpful in opening doors on behalf of individual firms. By traveling with executives from other, like-minded firms, managers can gain a wealth of valuable knowledge on markets and international business.

In addition to attending a trade fair or participating in a trade mission, there are various other important objectives to be achieved when visiting a target foreign market. First, a local visit will familiarize the visitor with potential customers, competitors, and macroconditions in the market, as well as provide a better understanding of what it will take to succeed in the market. Second, a visit provides the opportunity to better understand the type of intermediary needed to handle the firm's products. Such visits can also be used to actually negotiate potential supplier or distributor partnerships. Third, visiting the target country helps establish contacts with key local facilitators—including banks, government officials, and transportation companies—that can support international operations or augment the researcher's knowledge base.

Practical Considerations in Primary Data Collection

While primary data collection will yield new and valuable insights as the basis for informed decisions, it is not always practical because of cost or time constraints. Speed to market considerations may prompt managers to forgo primary data collection in such industries as fashion, publishing, entertainment, and computer software. Instead, companies may resort to alternative approaches.

The first alternative is direct experimentation. For example, in entering a new market, managers may simply initiate a small-scale effort to "test the waters." In this way, they can gather direct feedback from the market and use their learning as they evolve into a larger campaign. While U.S. and European companies tend to rely on formal research, Japanese companies are known for gaining insights through actual experience in the market. In Japan, companies tend to learn via direct interaction and experience in the marketplace, de-emphasizing upfront research. Thus, Western firms prefer "ready, aim, fire," whereas the Japanese emphasize "ready, fire, aim."

A second alternative to traditional primary data collection is for the firm to delegate responsibility for gathering market insights to its foreign partners. For example, many multinational firms rely on their foreign subsidiaries for local market knowledge and insights. Similarly, exporters often mobilize their distribution channel intermediaries and facilitators located in their foreign markets. For example, a foreign distributor can be charged with the task of validating and defining market potential and proposing alternative strategies for product adaptation, pricing, and retail distribution. Exporting firms that are physically removed from their foreign markets tend to rely on their distributors for information and guidance.

Interpretation of Insights Gained in the Proper Cultural and Social Context

Once suitable products and promising markets have been identified, managers conduct detailed market research on the characteristics of the target market, beyond developing a basic understanding of buyers, competitors, and the local business infrastructure. Characteristics of specific target markets are often more complex than expected due to deep-rooted and inscrutable aspects of culture, language, and other factors. Researchers may jump to conclusions that are consistent with their own customs, behaviors, and experiences, which, in reality, may be incorrect in the context of the foreign market. The researcher must take steps, therefore, to ensure that he or she acquires a genuine understanding of the mindset and habits of foreign buyers and how they perceive and use products.

The basic concept of products and their functions may be seen differently abroad. Basic notions such as beauty, youth, wealth, morality, happiness, and sex appeal vary greatly. Attitudes differ regarding such areas as housework, food preparation, clothing styles, child care, and personal hygiene. For example, the market for do-it-yourself car repair and maintenance products in Japan is limited because consumers tend to hire qualified professionals to do such work. In some nations, coffee is the usual morning beverage, whereas people in other countries favor tea, and some populations drink neither. Notions about offerings such as financial services, life insurance, bicycles, kitchen appliances, and personal recreation equipment vary from country to country.

Food for Thought: A Three-Phase Approach to Conducting International Market Research

International market research is particularly rewarding when pursued in a logical, step-by-step manner. In the sections that follow, we provide a framework of international market research, highlighting three layers of understanding: the macroenvironmental, microeconomic, and the cultural analysis levels.

The Macroenvironmental Analysis Phase

In the first phase of international market research, the marketer should collect information and analyze data on the key macroenvironmental dimensions summarized here. Data regarding each dimension is collected for each country's market that is under consideration.

- *Geographic factors* include the size of the country and topographical and climatic conditions. For example, the location of the Philippines in the middle of many Asia-Pacific routes makes it an ideal location for distribution, but the country's 7,000 islands also pose distribution challenges.
- *Demographic characteristics* include the size and the average annual growth rate of the market's population, population density and shape of its population pyramid, life expectancy, infant

and adolescent mortality, and urban versus rural population density.

- *Economic factors* include various measures of the country's economic strength, measured typically by gross domestic product (GDP) per capita, annual economic growth rate, urban versus rural income distribution, growth rates in manufacturing and services, and the nature of regulations regarding business activities.
- *Educational factors* include adult literacy, proportion of the population with a college degree, number of doctorates granted by educational institutions, and proportion of Internet users in the country.
- *Political factors* include the government system and frequency of government changes, attitudes toward foreign business, and the level of political stability.
- *Legal indicators* include import-export incentives and restrictions, ownership restrictions and local content legislation, government standards on products and processes, regulations such as those on the environment, patents and trademarks, and price controls.
- *Financial indicators* include inflation and unemployment rates, incentives for and restrictions on capital flows, exchange controls and exchange rate stability, and foreign exchange risk.
- *Technological factors* include existing technological stock of the country and opportunities for technology development, and currently available technological skills.

One approach is to develop an index in which each of the dimensions that are relevant to the marketer's objectives are represented. The marketer then weights each factor according to its relative importance. For each country of interest, each of the dimensions is then rated, and multiplied by the relevant weight. All of the weighted rating values are then added up, to obtain a total score for each country. An illustration of this type of analysis is provided by the Market Potential Indicators Index at globalEDGE™ (www.globaledge.msu.edu). This index provides a macropicture of market potential in emerging country markets based on the following variables: market size (20% weight), market growth rate (12%), market intensity (14%), market consumption capacity (10%), commercial infrastructure (14%), economic freedom (10%), market receptivity (12%), and country risk (8%).

Other approaches might use population density, urbanization, life expectancy, income distribution, lifestyle patterns, ethnic diversity, human development, and other variables, depending on the industry and what the firm aims to accomplish. The key task is to develop an index that is most relevant to the specific decision situation at hand. The value of this approach is that it allows the marketer to analyze each potential market using a systematic, *quantitative* approach that simplifies the decision process, allowing the researcher to evaluate the merits of each market.

The Microeconomic Analysis Phase

Having broadly painted a picture of the market of interest in the first phase, in the *second* phase, the marketer collects and analyzes data on

- competitiveness of the country's firms;
- intensity of competitive rivalry in the market; and
- presence or absence of industrial clusters in the market that can provide the firm with competitive advantages, such as product development skills or low labor costs.

The philosophy behind collecting this type of data is based on the importance of assessing the current and potential strengths and weaknesses of competitors present in the market, in order to devise appropriate competitor-oriented strategies and tactics. Intelligence about competitors' products, pricing practices, and distribution patterns is instrumental to the firm in developing its own strategic responses. In addition, highly competitive markets are generally better equipped to accept foreign products, services, and technology. Finally, analyzing the presence and nature of industrial clusters, and the nature of comparative advantages in the marketplace, helps the firm to understand how it can best employ assets in the market in order to maximize organizational performance.

One useful framework for obtaining information on the variables indicated above is the annual rankings compiled by the World Economic Forum (WEF). The WEF's rankings are based on the view that there is a direct relationship between the quality of a country's business environment and the sophistication of its companies' operations, competitiveness, and strategy. Developed by Michael Porter (1990), this perspective argues that a market environment's competitive prowess is a function of a diamond whose vertices are factor conditions (presence of high-quality, specialized inputs available to firms), demand conditions (presence of sophisticated and demanding local consumers), related and supporting industries (access to capable, locally based suppliers and firms in related fields and presence of clusters of industries instead of isolated industries), and context for firm strategy and rivalry (open and vigorous competition among rivals and a local context that encourages investment and sustained upgrading). Porter argues that these factors encourage an environment with strong companies and the ability to prosper economically.

Some of the important, more fine-grained variables that might be investigated in the microeconomic phase of analysis include the costs of importing foreign parts and supplies, overall infrastructure quality, local supplier competitiveness, effectiveness of antitrust policy, venture capital availability, open and hidden trade barriers, value-chain presence of foreign firms, buyer sophistication, local equity market access, capacity for innovation, and quality of financial, labor, and human resource markets.

The WEF's approach provides a holistic overview of the microeconomic "quality" of the market environment in a country based on factors that are critical to driving productivity and competitiveness in that market. A microeconomic analysis such as this allows the marketer to rank the country markets that it is considering, from most to least preferred, based on the efficiency and effectiveness of the markets' institutions, industries, and firms. In a recent ranking of 131 countries, the WEF ranked the United States as the most competitive country, followed by Switzerland, Denmark, Sweden, and Germany. Japan was ranked 8th, Korea 11th, France 18th, Malaysia 24th, and China 34th. India was ranked 48th, Russia 58th, and Brazil 72nd.

The Cultural Analysis Phase

In the final phase, the firm conducts research to better understand each market's cultural makeup and how elements of that cultural composition shape personal and societal values in the market, to the extent that these affect the firm's business activities there. One approach available to the researcher in this phase is to employ any of the cultural profiling methods developed by scholars such as Hofstede (1980, 2001), Schwartz (1992), Inglehart (1997), or House, Hanges, Javidan, Dorfman, and Gupta (2004).

For example, the dimensions of cultural orientation proposed by Hofstede (1980) provide a tool to interpret cultural differences and a foundation for classifying countries. By using the Hofstede framework, the manager can gain a deeper understanding of the cultural environment of a market by examining it in terms of five major dimensions, which are summarized here.

"Individualism versus collectivism" refers to whether the average person in a given culture functions primarily as an individual or within a group. In individualistic societies, ties among people are relatively loose, and each person tends to focus on his or her own self-interest. These societies prefer individualism over group conformity. Competition for resources is the norm, and those who compete best are rewarded financially. Australia, Canada, the United Kingdom, and the United States are examples of individualistic societies. By contrast, in collectivist societies, ties among individuals are more important than individualism. Business is conducted in the context of a group in which others' views are strongly considered. The group is all-important, as life is fundamentally a cooperative experience. Conformity and compromise help maintain group harmony. China, Japan, Panama, and South Korea are examples of strongly collectivist societies.

"Power distance" describes how a society deals with the inequalities in power that exist among people. Societies characterized by high power distance are relatively indifferent to inequalities and allow them to grow over time. There are substantial gaps between the powerful and the weak. Guatemala, Malaysia, the Philippines, and several Middle Eastern countries are examples of countries that exhibit high power distance. In contrast, in societies with low power distance, the gaps between the powerful and the weak are minimal. For example, in Scandinavian countries, such as Denmark and Sweden, governments institute tax and social welfare systems that ensure their nationals are relatively equal in terms of income and power. The United States scores relatively low on power distance. Social stratification affects power distance. In Japan, almost everyone belongs to the middle class, while in India the upper stratum controls most of the decision making and buying power. In companies, the degree of centralization of authority and autocratic leadership determines power distance. In high–power distance firms, autocratic management styles focus power at the top and grant little autonomy to lower level employees. In low–power distance firms, managers and subordinates are more equal and cooperate more to achieve organizational goals.

"Uncertainty avoidance" refers to the extent to which people can tolerate risk and uncertainty in their lives. People in societies with high uncertainty avoidance create institutions that minimize risk and ensure financial security. Companies emphasize stable careers and produce many rules to regulate worker actions and minimize ambiguity. Managers may be slow to make decisions and may investigate the nature and potential outcomes of several possible options. Belgium, France, and Japan are countries that score high on uncertainty avoidance. Societies that score low on uncertainty avoidance socialize their members to accept and become accustomed to uncertainty. Managers are entrepreneurial and relatively comfortable about taking risks, and make decisions relatively quickly. People accept each day as it comes and take their jobs in stride because they are less concerned about ensuring their future. They tend to tolerate behavior and opinions different from their own because they do not feel threatened by them. India, Ireland, Jamaica, and the United States are leading examples of countries with low uncertainty avoidance.

"Masculinity versus femininity" refers to a society's orientation relative to traditional male and female values. Masculine cultures tend to value competitiveness, assertiveness, ambition, and the accumulation of wealth. They are characterized by men and women who are assertive and focused on career and earning money. Examples include Australia and the United States. Hispanic cultures are relatively masculine and display a zest for action, daring, and competitiveness. In business, the masculinity dimension manifests as self-confidence, proactiveness, and leadership. Conversely, in feminine cultures, such as the Scandinavian countries, both men and women emphasize nurturing roles, interdependence among people, and caring for less fortunate people. Welfare systems are highly developed and education is subsidized.

"Long-term versus short-term orientation" denotes the degree to which people and organizations defer gratification to achieve long-term success. That is, firms and people in cultures with a long-term orientation tend to take the long view to planning and living. They focus on years and decades, instead of weeks or months. The long-term dimension is best illustrated by the so-called Asian values—traditional cultural orientations of several Asian societies such as China, Japan, and Singapore. Additional values associated with long-term orientation include discipline, loyalty, hard work, regard for education, esteem for the family, focus on group harmony, and control over one's desires. In contrast, the United States and most other Western countries tend to emphasize a short-term orientation.

Based on the results of surveys in 65 countries, Inglehart's approach (1997) found that all societies progress through three phases as they become economically advanced: premodern, modern, and postmodern. Inglehart hypothesizes that in the initial stage, as a society is advancing in economic terms, consumer behavior is based on values mainly related to basic survival. Here, consumer behavior is driven primarily by values such as family security and safety, and people purchase goods that ensure basic needs for themselves and their families. As the country evolves into a modern society, its consumers become more concerned about the well-being of others and will balance personal and family needs with the needs of others. When the society becomes postmodern, it focuses on rational values and is much more willing to share its wealth with others. In Inglehart's research, many African and some Latin American countries fall into the premodern societies group. By contrast, Sweden, Norway, Denmark, Germany, Finland, Switzerland, and the Netherlands fall into the postmodern category. All other countries in Inglehart's research, including the United States, France, Canada, Australia, and Italy, fall into the modern group in between the pre- and postmodern categories.

In summary, firms that contemplate entry into or operating in particular markets should develop a deeper understanding of those markets via analysis of, and learning about, their macro-, micro-, and cultural environments. Much of this research can be performed using secondary data sources. However, deeper analyses demand that data be collected directly from buyers, or other relevant entities, via primary research. When obtaining primary data, the marketer conducts surveys and then analyzes and interprets findings from those surveys. However, research to obtain primary data is fraught with difficulties, which we will discuss in the next chapter.

CHAPTER 5

Methodological Considerations in International Market Research

Researchers face unique challenges in gathering reliable data and information in international markets. The quality and reliability of data are critically important because of the stakes involved. Table 5.1 identifies common challenges faced by international market researchers when collecting primary data.

We will now address each of the issues in Table 5.1 in turn. Access is often a major concern in international research. To obtain reliable answers to many types of research questions, the researcher must venture into the field and interact with potential buyers or other subjects of interest. For example, when Avon began selling cosmetics in Japan, it had to interview numerous typical housewives in order to gauge their habits regarding cosmetic usage and their receptivity to receiving door-to-door sales personnel in their homes. When trying to understand the insurance needs of people in China, the insurance giant AIG sent researchers into the field in various Chinese cities to survey Chinese people about their insurance needs. When seeking to market pharmaceuticals in Latin America, GlaxoSmithKline interviewed random samples of elderly people from various Latin American countries.

How do researchers access such diverse groups? First, they must ensure the right subjects are targeted for investigation. Subjects may be found among government officials, channel intermediaries, local managers, employees, retail consumers, and buyers within highly specific market segments. Second, the researcher must be aggressive in finding and gaining

Table 5.1   Key Challenges in International Market Research

THE ISSUE OF CONCERN	CHALLENGE	HOW TO RESOLVE THE ISSUE
Access	When surveying subjects in the market of interest, how can we access the most suitable subjects in terms of age, income, or other characteristics?	Target appropriate subjects and be persistent in securing their responses.
Representativeness	Are the sampled subjects typical of the population under study?	Carefully assess the profile of the sampled subjects regarding key characteristics of interest, such as age, income, buying habits.
Conceptual equivalence	Do the concepts of interest exist, or are they understood in the same way, in the market(s) of interest?	Cultural or country specific concepts (e.g., "saving face," "customer orientation") should be investigated to see how they can be accurately expressed in the target market, or avoided altogether.
Translation equivalence	Will the respondents in different markets attribute equivalent meaning to the same question, as expressed in the original English?	Use *back translation* to ensure equivalence. First, have the question translated from the original language by a bilingual translator who is a native speaker of the target language. Then, have the target language version translated back into the original language by a bilingual who is a native speaker of the original language. Finally, compare the back-translated version to the original version to check for errors and quality of translation. Make corrections as needed.
Construct validity	To what extent do the study results actually measure what they are supposed to measure? Do the collected data represent a valid measure of the concepts or constructs of interest?	Take steps to ensure that measurement scales correctly represent the concepts and constructs of interest.
Reliability	Can the same results be obtained when measurements are taken on different occasions (consistency over time) or from different individuals (consistency across respondents)?	Follow rigorous research methods, including careful design of surveys and measures, to ensure reliability is achieved.

(*continued on next page*)

Table 5.1   *Key Challenges in International Market Research*
(continued)

THE ISSUE OF CONCERN	CHALLENGE	HOW TO RESOLVE THE ISSUE
Incomplete or inconsistent findings	Are there substantial gaps or inconsistencies in the conclusions of separate studies conducted by different methods?	Use triangulation, in which the researcher compares results obtained from different procedures. For example, a survey should be tested on two different, smaller samples, before it is administered to the main study population. Convergent results will provide a degree of confidence in the accuracy of conclusions drawn.

access to appropriate subjects for addressing specific research questions. When it comes to collecting primary data internationally, the best researchers are intrepid and uninhibited. They go wherever the data can be found. Third, often researchers must be creative, with the ability to devise imaginative and resourceful solutions to securing the data.

Representativeness is the extent to which respondents are typical of the population under study. For example, when General Motors sought to sell trucks in Australia, it surveyed people living in rural areas as well as those working in the construction, agriculture, and similar industries—that is, people inclined to buy trucks. When researchers from the fast-food chain Burger King surveyed consumers in Latin America about their food needs and preferences, they sought people who were representative of actual fast-food consumers. Ensuring representativeness is critical because buyers vary by age, income level, buying habits, and other factors.

Conceptual equivalence refers to whether the concepts of interest exist, or are expressed in similar ways, in different countries and cultures. Concepts, such as "materialism," "timeliness," or "saving face," may not be relevant or not construed in the same way in different cultures (Craig & Douglas, 2005). The researcher should emphasize concepts that are well understood in given cultures as well as universal concepts that are not specific to any one culture. Such measures facilitate easier comparison and more straightforward communication. Alternatively, if the researcher is interested in concepts that are specific to a particular country (e.g., *guanxi* in

China, *jeito* in Brazil), then rigorous research methods must be applied in order to clearly understand and express those concepts accurately.

Translation equivalence refers to whether respondents in different countries will attribute equivalent meaning to the same question in a survey or similar instrument. The practice of translating questions *directly* from the original language to another without checking for the equivalence of meaning often leads to translation inaccuracies and blunders. For example, there is no direct equivalent in most languages for the commonly used Japanese word *mottai nai*, which can be translated variously as "wasteful," "it is unreasonable," "it's a shame not to use it," and "I do not deserve it." When Ajinomoto, a Japanese food company, measures the dimensions of taste that people prefer in its spicy products, respondents in different countries have differing opinions of what constitutes "sweet," "sour," "bitter," "salty," "spicy," and "bland." Taste is a very subjective concept, so researchers must assess responses with care.

Differences in meaning exist even among the various English-speaking countries. For example, the verb "to table" means to put an issue on hold in American English, but it means to take up an issue (the exact opposite) in British English. In American English, a "scheme" can mean "a somewhat devious plan," whereas in British English, a scheme is usually just "a plan." If Dell Corporation surveys online buyers across several European countries, it must translate its questionnaire into French, German, and Italian. If the translation is poor, then researchers may obtain subtly different answers to the same questions. There are countless other ways in which translation problems can threaten the validity of international research.

The recommended method for ensuring translation equivalence is *back translation*. Using this procedure, a questionnaire is translated from the source language—say English—by a bilingual translator who is a native speaker of the target language—say Italian—into which the translation is being made. Then the Italian version is translated back into English by another bilingual who is a native speaker of Italian. The two English versions of the questionnaire are then compared to check for errors and the quality of the translation (Craig & Douglas, 2005). Adjustments are then made to the original questionnaire as needed.

Broadly speaking, validity concerns the problem of whether a qu...
tionnaire or other research instrument is truly measuring what it intends
to measure. Construct validity refers to whether the data collected are
a valid measure of the construct of interest. A *construct* is a relatively
complex concept "constructed" of a collection of lesser concepts. For
example, "respondent age" is not a construct; it is a simple concept (in
fact, it is a *variable*), which can be easily measured by a simple question:
"How old are you?" By contrast, "product liking" is a relatively complex
concept, a *construct* that is best measured by using a collection of questions. For example, to obtain a proper assessment of a person's liking for
a particular product, it is usually insufficient to simply ask "How well do
you like this product?" Rather, the researcher will obtain a more robust
measure of such a construct by asking a series of questions, such as the
following:

I like this product in terms of its design	strongly disagree	1 2 3 4 5	strongly agree
I like this product in terms of its technology	strongly disagree	1 2 3 4 5	strongly agree
I like this product in terms of its performance	strongly disagree	1 2 3 4 5	strongly agree
I like this product in terms of its quality	strongly disagree	1 2 3 4 5	strongly agree
I like this product in terms of its features	strongly disagree	1 2 3 4 5	strongly agree
I like this product in terms of its packaging	strongly disagree	1 2 3 4 5	strongly agree

Collectively, the above questions do a much better job of measuring
"product liking" than simply asking "How well do you like this product?" Accordingly, a questionnaire is composed of (a) questions that
measure variables (e.g., "How old are you?") and (b) a series of scales,
each composed of two or more questions, that measure constructs.
The researcher needs to ensure that the measures used have high construct
validity—that is, that they successfully represent each construct. As
research progresses, the manager should continually ask: Is the research
measuring what it is supposed to measure? Relying on results of research

conducted incorrectly to make decisions can prove problematic at best and disastrous at worst.

Reliability refers to similarity of results as provided by independent but comparable measures of the same object or trait. It relates to whether research results can be applied to a wider group than those who took part in a study. Reliability is mainly concerned with making sure that the method of data gathering leads to consistent results. In this context, the researcher should ask: Would similar results be obtained if another group containing different respondents was used? For some types of research, reliability can be established by having different researchers follow the same methods to see if results can be duplicated. If results are similar, then the method of gathering data is likely to be reliable. In market research, reliability is valued because the marketer wants to ensure the results of the study will be exactly the same when repeated in different markets with similar populations tested. For example, if a questionnaire reveals that online buyers in Sydney like eBay.com because of its wide range of products, ease of payment, and user-friendliness, reliability in measurement is achieved when readers in Melbourne emphasize these same qualities in responding to the same questionnaire. Reliability is an indicator of the quality of questionnaires and other measuring instruments. Assessing reliability is a way of assuring that a given concept is measured with little or no error. The greater the reliability, the more confident the researcher can be of research findings. If the reliability of measurement varies across markets but is not detected, conclusions drawn from a cross-national study may be faulty. For example, what appears to be a cross-national difference in attitudes toward a product may in fact be a reflection of the variation in the reliability of the underlying measures employed in the research.

Incomplete or inconsistent findings refer to substantial gaps or inconsistencies in the conclusions of separate studies conducted by different methods. Often the researcher encounters conflicting conclusions in the findings of two or more studies conducted in an international setting. The differences in the findings may be attributable to diverse methods used by the original researchers, differences in the samples drawn, or using differing analysis methods. The dilemma is to how to make sense out of these studies by examining their relative merits and deficiencies. A skillful researcher may be able to arrive at a set of converging findings by carefully going through the studies. Convergence of results should provide a degree of confidence in the validity and reliability of conclusions drawn from the studies (Amine & Cavusgil, 1986).

Triangulation is the process of validating findings obtained from multiple sources or multiple research efforts. The term is derived from trigonometry, where it refers to a method for calculating the distance to a point by viewing it from two other points. Triangulation is particularly useful in international business because of the complex nature of foreign markets and the presence of often conflicting information. For example, if you want to understand consumer attitudes toward foreign-branded cars in Russia, you could interview managers in the Russian auto industry, conduct a survey among Russian car owners, or conduct a focus group with dealer salespeople. Alternatively, you could do all three and contrast the results. That is, you "triangulate" your findings from three studies, an approach that maximizes the validity of findings.

Giant Bicycle Inc. is a Taiwanese bicycle manufacturer that captured 5% of the retail market in China, which is estimated at 30 million bicycles per year. Prior to entering China, Giant conducted extensive market research, seeking to learn not only what people buy but also *which* segments of the population buy *what types* of products and *why*. Most bicycle manufacturers target the low end of Chinese consumers who shop on price. But Giant's research revealed a substantial segment of buyers who ride for fun, adventure, and exercise. Giant researched these attributes in China and designed various models around them, allowing it to charge higher prices. Because the Chinese market is huge and complex, Giant had a hard time drawing inferences from limited secondary data. Thus, the firm triangulated research from secondary sources as well as interviews with consumers and retailers, and by going to bicycle parking sites in cities, villages, and recreational areas to observe what bikes people use for different occasions (Crocker & Tay, 2004).

Resources and International Market Research

Managers need to invest sufficient resources to design and implement international research and interpret the findings. But international research can be costly. This is especially true when managers collect primary data.

Smaller firms may be disadvantaged when conducting international research because they tend to lack substantial resources. For most companies, the most important resources for market research are financial and human resources. Multicountry studies with original subjects are expensive. In-house research staff command substantial resources. Commissioning research to external market research agencies and coordinating such research in multiple countries is costly in terms of time, money, and managerial talent.

When conducting cross-cultural research for the first time, companies follow a learning curve. The curve is steep in the early stages, so the firm incurs costs in terms of time and money. As managers become more experienced, they gradually learn the most effective and economical ways to research foreign markets, competitors, and doing business abroad. The most experienced firms leverage information technology and build databases that incorporate a range of indicators. The most sophisticated firms leverage the extensive data available online from knowledge portals such as globalEDGE™ (www.globaledge.msu.edu).

You might wonder who carries out international research. In smaller firms, it is usually a single individual, typically an export manager, a global procurement specialist, or another person in charge of international business. In larger firms, several individuals may be available to collect, organize, and report critical information and intelligence to managerial staff, as well as provide advice on key choices that the firm has to make. Desk research is best conducted by individuals who have cross-national experience and at least some research expertise. Foreign language skills are a plus for much of the information that is sought from abroad.

When research capabilities are limited, or when the stakes are high, the company is likely to commission research to a professional market research firm. Such specialists can provide a range of research services and techniques. They may possess specialized knowledge on specific industries, countries, or world regions. Larger market research firms have networks of representative offices and affiliates abroad that provide extensive research support. These connections ensure maximal access to target populations around the world. Table 5.2 lists some of the leading international market research firms. These firms account for over half of annual spending on global commercial research.

Table 5.2   Top Global Research Firms

COMPANY	PARENT COUNTRY	INDUSTRY SPECIALIZATION
VNU N.V.	Netherlands	Retail, media, and the Internet
Taylor Nelson Sofres plc	United Kingdom	Automotive, consumer products and retail sales
IMS Health Inc.	United States	Health care
GfK AG	Germany	Retail, health care, and media
The Kantar Group	United Kingdom	Financial services, health care, and retail
Ipsos Group S.A.	France	Automotive, retail, and financial services
Information Resources Inc.	United States	Consumer packaged goods
Synovate	United Kingdom	Automotive, financial services, and health care
Westat Inc.	United States	Health care, energy, and education
Arbitron Inc.	United States	Media and advertising
INTAGE Inc.	Japan	Transportation and travel, distribution, and health care
Harris Interactive Inc.	United States	Consumer goods, health care, and transportation
Maritz Research	United States	Automotive, financial services, and telecommunications
J. D. Power and Associates	United States	Automotive, telecommunications, travel, and real estate
Video Research Ltd.	United States	Media and advertising

Source: Honomichl, J. (2006, August 15). Honomichl global top 25. *Marketing News,* 20.

Larger market research firms can deal with the many complex tasks, including selecting the sample of buyers or other representative subjects, as well as the design of research instruments, data analysis, and interpretation. Market research firms are equipped to carry out more complex projects, such as long-term studies and focus groups involving different groups of buyers. Companies employ market research firms particularly when they are considering a complex or expensive foreign entry, often involving foreign direct investment.

In addition to providing customized market research services, some research firms also provide panel data on a subscription basis to users. These firms, specialized in a particular industry, compile data from individual companies that make up the industry, aggregate and organize data, and then make them available to users on a continuing basis. For example, several leading research firms serve the global pharmaceutical industry by providing data, trends, insights, and networking opportunities for thousands of firms.

While the services of market research firms are often costly, government agencies and industry support organizations can provide similar information for little or no cost. Examples include International Trade Canada (www.infoexport.gc.ca), Department of Foreign Affairs and Trade in Australia (www.austrade.gov.au), the Ministry of Trade and Industry in Norway (www.nortrade.com), and the International Trade Administration in the United States (www.doc.gov). These agencies offer country and industry market reports, customized market research services, in-country feasibility studies, and various region-specific programs, as well as trade missions and fairs. A particularly useful resource is the International Trade Centre, a subsidiary of the World Trade Organization (www.intracen.org/index.htm). This organization, based in Geneva, Switzerland, provides free technical assistance to companies from the developing world and offers a broad range of reference material and guidance on international trade.

In addition to contacting home government sources, the international researcher can investigate *foreign* government sources, since they are likely to know the situation in their own countries better than others would. However, the best research data is derived from multiple sources, both domestic and international. State, provincial, and national governments in many countries are good resources for obtaining data and intelligence, help with international business plans, seminars on doing business abroad, venues for reporting unfair trade practices, opportunities to bid on major international projects, programs for finding foreign intermediaries, and tax incentives, as well as loans, loan guarantees, and other financial support. For example, the Japanese government often counsels foreign firms on entering the Japanese market through its principal trade promotion agency, the Japan External Trade Organization (JETRO; www.jetro .go.jp).

International research is most useful when blended with sound managerial judgment. The researcher should always seek to understand the reason behind events and bare facts. To anticipate and grasp future developments, managers need to know not only *what* is happening, but also *why* it is happening. They should investigate the implications of current and past trends on sales and other activities in the market. Ultimately, market research lays the foundation for success in international business.

Food for Thought: Measurement Issues in International Market Research

One of the key challenges in international market research is the measurement of specific constructs and the variables that underlie them. To illustrate these issues, we will use the example of one important construct in international business—the country-of-origin (CO) cue associated with a product and often communicated via a "Made in _____" label. CO often affects whether a consumer will buy a certain car, wine, clothing, or other product. For example, most people are more inclined to buy a television made in Japan than a television made in Mexico. They are more likely to buy a car made in Germany than a car made in China. For some products, CO can even overwhelm other relevant cues—such as brand image and price—and deter customer purchase. In the consumer's mind, the CO image may be composed of multiple variables, such as the consumer's stereotyping of that country's people (e.g., "Japanese people are hardworking") and products in general (e.g., "German products are made with meticulous workmanship").

When the researcher sets out to measure CO, he or she must ensure that the construct is measured accurately and comprehensively. In these circumstances, various measurement concerns arise, especially regarding *reliability* and *validity*. Weak levels of reliability can be caused by many inputs, including faulty research design, sampling flaws, response-related deficiencies, scaling imperfections, and a myriad of other factors, such as functional and conceptual inequivalencies encountered in research. One can establish the degree of reliability achieved in a research project (the higher, the better) in a number of ways, but the most popular of these are test-retest and internal consistency. Test-retest allows the researcher to confirm through multiple attempts that the findings achieved in initial attempt(s) are corroborated by those achieved in later attempts. Internal consistency permits the researcher to verify that variables (or subconstructs) composing a construct show high levels of consistency.

Researchers gauge this by examining inter-item correlations and item-to-total correlations in a scale. Such correlation values can be obtained by assessing scales using statistical analysis software, such as AMOS, SAS, or SPSS. These reveal how well the variables that compose the construct are related to one another and how well they, taken together, compose a single construct, such as the CO image of a product.

Establishing validity assists the researcher in substantiating that the construct under scrutiny—say CO image—is in fact measuring that image and not some other phenomenon—say brand image or value image. While researchers are typically concerned with many different types of validity, the most important types in market research are construct validity and content validity. We defined construct validity earlier. Content validity is simply the degree to which an operationalization of a construct represents the concept about which generalizations are to be made. If, for example, CO image is operationalized in a study as being composed of people image and product image, and these are operationalized via questions that tap these subconstructs well, we would be confident that the CO image construct in our research has high content validity. Content and construct validities are different in that content validity is concerned with whether the operationalization of a construct, such as CO image, is a true *representation* of the concept about which generalizations are being made, while construct validity focuses on determining whether an operationalization of a construct truly *measures* that construct.

Construct validity is established in at least three ways: convergent, discriminant, and nomological validity. Convergent validity measures the degree to which multiple attempts at measuring the concept through different methods are in agreement. Typically measured through the correlation between the multiple attempts, a high correlation coefficient (usually 90% or more) indicates that convergent validity has been achieved.

In contrast, discriminant validity measures the extent to which a concept differs from other concepts in our research—that is, the degree to which measures of different concepts are distinct. If two or more concepts are truly unique, then valid measures of each of these should *not* correlate highly. For example, if CO image, brand image, and value image are in fact different constructs, they should not correlate highly for us to conclude that we have discriminant validity in our research. In the same vein, if attitudes toward a country and its people and those toward its products in general are two separate constructs, then they should not be related highly for us to conclude that we have achieved discriminant validity.

Nomological validity is the extent to which predictions based on the concept that what a research instrument (e.g., a scale used in a consumer survey) purports to measure are confirmed with actual data. For example, if the researcher used a standard scale with which to measure consumer ethnocentrism and found that (a) the stronger one's ethnocentrism is, the more likely one is to purchase an American-made car; and that (b) if more-ethnocentric consumers display less favorable attitudes toward foreign-made cars than less ethnocentric consumers, then these two results, combined, would provide support for the nomological validity of the consumer ethnocentrism concept and its measurement via the consumer ethnocentrism scale used by the researcher (Shimp & Sharma, 1987).

In measuring CO image, the researcher would seek high degrees of convergent, discriminant, and nomological validity. A high degree of convergent validity would assure that high correlations exist among the subcomponents that compose this image—that is, people image and products in general image. Discriminant validity would underscore that low correlations exist among people image, brand image, and value image, each one serving as a discriminator of purchase intentions to one degree or another. Nomological validity would show that findings obtained from data analyses are in agreement with expected measures. That is, the research scales would demonstrate integrity.

At least two additional measures of validity are important in international market research. First, establishing external validity—that is removing experimenter and setting bias from conclusions so that generalizations can be made across populations and across research settings—is a critical task. When conducting research cross-nationally, researchers sometimes unintentionally bias findings by providing cues to their subjects; in some cases, the research setting itself (focus group setting, shopping mall intercept, face-to-face interview, etc.) can influence the subject's willingness to respond in ways that he perceives as what is expected of him (socially desirable responses). Also, cultural or national differences in response patterns (extreme response styles, tendencies to yea- or nay-say, midpoint responding, etc.) can contaminate research findings and threaten the validity of conclusions drawn from market research data. As each of these can introduce bias into the researchers' analysis and confound her findings, the researcher should seek to eliminate these from final generalizations (de Jong, Steenkamp, Fox, & Baumgartner, 2008).

Second, scale dimensionality needs to be established—that is, the scales used to operationalize the construct under consideration should reflect the hypothesized dimensionality of the scale. If, for example, a scale developed to measure the degree of ethnocentrism possessed by consumers in a given market is hypothesized to possess a unidimensional factor structure, it is incumbent on the researcher to confirm that this is, indeed, the case. That is, the researcher must show that the ethnocentrism scale used in her research is truly a measure of consumer ethnocentrism and not one composed of ethnocentrism plus other constructs—say of economic nationalism, animosity toward the country of origin of the product, patriotism, social identity, and so on—which might dilute the marketer's understanding of the level of ethnocentrism in that market (Netemeyer, Bearden, & Sharma, 2003).

Establishing scale unidimensionality is also important because it is assumed that the scale's empirical factor structure is reflective of its conceptual dimensionality theorized by the researcher. This is a prerequisite to establishing reliability and validity in one's research. Scale unidimensionality is assessed typically by the analysis of data through a technique called "factor analysis"; both exploratory and confirmatory factor analyses are used (Gerbing & Anderson, 1988).

Establishing equivalencies presents another set of challenges to the researcher. Knowledge and familiarity with the constructs that we measure may vary across cultural groups. For example, subjects in different markets may possess different understandings of certain concepts: they may be illiterate; they may be unfamiliar with certain research instruments (e.g., surveys or focus groups); they may be used to different measurement units; and they may have different expectations about who should or should not express opinions about a topic, make a choice, or engage in an actual purchase. For example, "comfort" in a car may mean one thing to an American driver, another to a Brazilian driver, and yet another to a Tanzanian driver. "Perceived risk" in making a purchase may mean different things to different consumers depending on their abilities to buy, the choices available to them, decisions they must make among purchase options, and their social settings or social standing.

The researcher may encounter several other equivalency problems. Consumers' responses are based on a blend of emotions and rational motives, and these may vary across cultural groups. Cultural standards that are used in making product attributions may vary as well. To overcome equivalency problems, the marketer needs to understand the degree to which cognitions and beliefs are used in consumers' attributions about the marketer's product in each market. Furthermore, the number and composition of significant beliefs about a product, relevant values that drive a purchase, and even propensities for value change may vary across cultures. These make the marketer's identification of relevant belief sets and attitudes at work in a purchase situation difficult.

When measuring beliefs, attitudes, purchase intentions, and purchase behavior in each market, it is important to ensure correspondence in such drivers as action (e.g., "buy" versus "not buy"), target product (e.g., "Toyota Camry"), context (e.g., "for the family"), and time (e.g., "within the next month"). Different markets are likely to follow different paths to ensure correspondence among these, or they may be comfortable with some incongruence among them. The mental processes that consumers use to integrate existing attitudes with personality characteristics, cognitive styles, and social contexts, and the way that they blend these in responding to survey instruments, may also vary, adding barriers to the researcher's interpretation task. Thus, it is essential to account for these equivalency issues when conducting, and drawing conclusions from, cross-national research.

Perhaps the most significant equivalence that the researcher needs to establish, however, is construct equivalence. Here, the researcher needs to confirm that the phenomenon actually exists across the country markets under her microscope, that culture-specific issues have been accounted for, and that culture-specific measures are, in fact, used while making cross-cultural comparisons (Craig & Douglas, 2005). In this context, the researcher needs to determine that there is conceptual, functional, and category equivalence. It is paramount that subjects have equal understanding and interpretation of the concepts under consideration. For example, attachment to one's possessions (materialism) or love for one's country (patriotism) might evoke different images and different emotions in different markets. Personality traits that are relevant in one country (e.g., assertiveness, gregariousness, agreeableness) may not be relevant in other countries.

Functional equivalence refers to equal concept operationalization by consumers across markets—that is, whether functions or attributes of products are perceived in similar ways across markets. For example, a bicycle might perform recreational, athletic, and transportation functions for suburban, mountain area, and college student markets, respectively. Beer may be served as an alcoholic beverage in some countries (Northern Europe) while as a soft drink in others (Mediterranean Europe). Mayonnaise may be served as a sandwich spread in the United States but as a salad dressing in Thailand, and so on.

Establishing equivalence is also important in ascertaining the credibility, generalizability, and comparability of research findings. Confirming who responded to the survey, whether this response was voluntary, and verifying whether the forthcoming data were complete are important data collection equivalency tasks. In some countries, for example, expression of opinion may be considered inappropriate for certain groups of people. In a focus group in Japan, young people are less inclined to speak their minds if older peers are present. In Islamic countries, it is often difficult to elicit opinions from women.

Validating that the respondents understood the concepts intended, that these had similar levels of valence, and that respondents' interpretations were consistent over time are important respondent interpretation tasks. Authenticating that there are no variations among national samples' "do not know" or "no opinion" responses to a question, or accounting for these differences is another important undertaking in corroborating response bias in cross-cultural research efforts.

Another challenge is establishing sampling equivalence. This task involves assuring that sampling frames and the sampling units drawn in different countries are contextually equal. For example, if urban housewives are used as subjects in one country, every effort should be made to use urban housewives in the other country markets where research is being conducted. If extended family members are involved in a given purchase situation in one country, then similar family members should be involved in the purchase situations in other countries.

Establishing metric equivalence is also important. This involves measuring the objects of interest—whether these are attitudes, beliefs, intentions, or behaviors—with the same research instrument in each country. Ensuring metric equivalence helps assure that subjects in different national samples are responding to the measurement scales in the same manner. Unfamiliarity with certain scales or scoring formats in some markets may cause inequivalencies that need to be corrected before drawing conclusions from international studies. For example, if consumers who are expressing opinions about a purchase are unfamiliar with a particular scaling method, then they may not respond to the questions of interest with integrity.

Another variant, translation equivalence, involves validating that the items that make up the research instrument are translated with fidelity so that they carry the same meaning across markets. One way to assure this is through the back-translation method, explained earlier.

The researcher must finally establish operational (or administrative) equivalence—that is, the conduct of the researchers in experimental situations should be similar across markets. In a survey research situation, researchers in each market setting should administer the survey in similar fashion, the same kind of administrator should be involved in running the survey, and opinion expression situations should not vary. For example, if research is being administered in a shopping mall by young college students in one country, it should be administered by similar persons in a similar setting in the other countries in which research is being conducted.

Paying sufficient attention to the issues addressed in this chapter will ensure that data and findings obtained from international market research are reliable, valid, and generalizable to populations of interest, and therefore lead to more accurate conclusions about the behavior of consumers in multiple markets.

CHAPTER 6

The Research Process
and an Example

Objective fact-finding provides the means to address informational needs and accumulate new knowledge. Much knowledge is acquired through processes internal to the firm, drawing liberally from the accumulated experience and insights of its own employees. But knowledge can also be obtained by careful investigation of market conditions and competitors' behavior. The character and complexity of research is a function of the experience of the firm and the nature of its international activities. Beginner firms investigate a range of issues, while firms with existing foreign operations investigate specific and complex issues, such as where to locate new manufacturing or research and development (R&D) facilities and what new products to offer in foreign markets.

For example, hoping to increase its sales in the United States, the German firm Volkswagen (VW) launched an ambitious program of market research. VW's team of 23 researchers lived for 18 months in the United States, traveling widely to visit such venues as the Mall of America, the Coca-Cola museum, a rodeo, a drag race, and the spring-break beaches of Florida. The goals were to better understand the market and their competitors, establish new market objectives, and develop new products. The team systematically tried every form of U.S. transportation, including subways, rental cars, and red-eye flights. They drove a different vehicle of competing carmakers every week. Largely schooled in making cars for Europe, the team eventually learned what makes the U.S. car market distinctive. For example, U.S. drivers like storage space and music speakers. They use their cars to drive family members around and get to lunches and social occasions. They consider cars an expression of personal independence. VW used the resulting knowledge to develop new vehicles for the U.S. market ("VW's American," 2006).

When the firm conducts marketing research, its goal is to acquire deep understanding of a problem with as little error as possible. For example, when a food marketer such as Kellogg considers the introduction of a new breakfast cereal into a market, it will want to know which cereal products the market can absorb and how the product's concept (e.g., healthy, promotion of fitness) can be differentiated from competing products already available in the market. The researcher also may want to determine the targets that most likely will consume the product, the dimensions of consumer behavior that Kellogg managers can use to profile these consumers, and the most likely projections for sales in the market. While searching for answers to these questions, Kellogg researchers will likely know that there will be errors in the judgments that they make in answering these questions, and they will want to minimize these errors.

The Research Process

When conducting broad market research, the research process follows a series of steps summarized in Figure 6.1. We will elaborate on this research process in the pages that follow.

Step 1: Identify the Problem

At this stage the researcher defines the purpose of the research, the boundaries of the problem, and the specific research questions to be answered. The researcher decides what knowledge is required, in order to focus on well-defined, specific issues. This stage involves asking the questions such as the following:

- What information do we already know?
- What information do we need to find out?
- What sources of information do we need to use?
- How will we analyze, report, and use the information gathered?

Identifying the problem in this way lays the foundation for the remainder of the research process. It notifies managers and other stakeholders about the goals, details, and urgency of the research project. This understanding

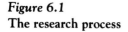

Figure 6.1
The research process

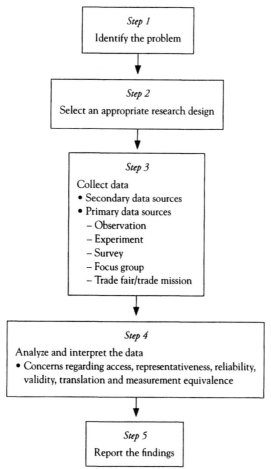

helps to determine the decisions to be made when it comes to planning and implementing the research.

Step 2: Select an Appropriate Research Design

The investigator chooses a research design that best addresses the research question(s) identified in Step 1. This involves deciding on the appropriate measurement scales and research instruments to use (e.g., a consumer survey), and selecting the appropriate sample (e.g., "families living in urban areas with children at home"). Care should be taken to choose a representative sample(s) that generates findings that can be generalized to the markets of interest, aiming to ensure externally valid findings. Selecting the appropriate research design may also involve developing hypotheses that help to address the specific research questions that the researcher has developed.

Step 3: Collect Data

The researcher collects data that is relevant to the research question(s) at hand. The data must be of sufficient quality and specificity to properly address the research question(s) identified in Step 1. Data may be collected from secondary sources or from primary data sources, via techniques such as observation, experiments, surveys, and focus groups, or by participating in a trade fair or a trade mission. The researcher begins by collecting secondary data and then moves on to collecting primary data as research questions become more specific. Obtaining high quality data is one of the biggest challenges in international research. If the researcher obtains inaccurate or misleading data, then resultant conclusions will be incorrect.

Step 4: Analyze and Interpret the Data

Interpreting findings and reaching conclusions are usually the most difficult phases in the research process. Considerable wisdom and experience are needed to ensure insightful analysis and to generate recommendations for management action. The nature and complexity of the data and the availability of time dictate the degree of sophistication of data analysis and interpretation. Data analysis techniques vary, from simple, qualitative analysis to more rigorous statistical analysis. As explained in the previous chapter, in the course of collecting and analyzing data, the researcher is concerned about access, representativeness, reliability, validity, translation, and measurement equivalence. In this stage the researcher tabulates, summarizes, and draws inferences from the data. Data analysis is often performed using a specialized software designed for this purpose, such as SPSS or SAS.

Step 5: Report the Findings

At this stage, the researcher creates a written report that summarizes study results and makes relevant recommendations, which are then reported to management in the firm. The preparation of appropriate reports and presentation materials is critical for communicating findings to senior management and other stakeholders. Senior managers can be overwhelmed with the amount of reports and information that they receive each day, and so creating the optimum type of report to ensure reader attention and comprehension is a critical step in the research process. Conclusions and recommendations generated from market research can be both periodic and one-time-only reports. The information contained in research findings is critical for making appropriate business decisions and for justifying given courses of action.

An Extended Example of the Research Process

Let's illustrate the research process with an example. Suppose that Acme Motor Company (AMC) is an automaker based in the United States. AMC wants to market its line of fuel-efficient cars to Europe. Management has decided to target France as AMC's first market, with a view to expanding into other European countries later. Note that firms new to international business often begin first by entering a single country, where they refine their marketing efforts, before expanding into other countries or into a larger, regional marketplace. In our example, AMC wants to market its Cruiser line of inexpensive cars, at a selling price of less than $10,000. Suppose also that, simultaneously, an Indian car company, Tata Motors, has announced that it also will begin selling its fuel-efficient subcompact Nano car in various European countries, including France.

Problem Identification

AMC researchers view the basic problems and research questions as follows:

1. Identify one or more appropriate market segments in France for the Cruiser brand.

2. Acquire an understanding of the strategies and tactics necessary to best position and market the Cruiser to the segment(s) identified in France, in order to generate maximum profits within 3 years.

3. Acquire a market share of at least 5% of the French car market within 5 years.

4. Given that Europeans prefer European-branded cars, Acme wants to find out about French consumers' perceptions of automobiles made in the United States. What approaches should AMC follow to minimize the effects of any negative perceptions?

5. What features do French consumers in the identified segment(s) prefer most when buying a new car? What perceptions, beliefs, and attitudes are most influential when French consumers buy cars?

6. What other car brands compete with the Cruiser in France? What are the major features and attributes of these competing brands? What car features and other variables can be used to differentiate the Cruiser from the Nano, the Indian brand by Tata Motors?

7. Regarding tactical marketing issues, what is the appropriate level of pricing for Cruiser models? What advertising would be most appropriate for the Cruiser in France?

8. To what extent can Cruiser cars, pricing, branding, communications, and distribution be standardized for the French and other, future markets in Europe?

Regarding the last question, in order to minimize costs and reap other advantages, firms such as AMC usually prefer to "standardize" the products that they offer for sale abroad. Companies prefer to sell the same or similar products, using the same pricing, distribution, and advertising throughout major world markets. At the same time, however, some product features must be adapted to suit conditions in individual countries. For example, the owner's manual that accompanies the Cruiser must be written in the language of the target market (in this case, French), and pricing must be adjusted to suit local purchasing power. Managers conduct market research to ascertain the product features and other marketing program elements that they can standardize, and those that they must adapt. In our example, AMC wants to find out the extent to which it can standardize marketing elements in France and across Europe, and the degree to which the elements must be adapted to the needs of individual European countries. Ultimately, AMC needs to strike the right balance between standardization and adaptation of its cars. Part of its market research seeks to find this balance.

Research Design

After framing the research problems and questions, AMC managers develop the research design. In order to minimize research costs, data initially will be sought from secondary sources. Researchers decide to collect secondary data by combing through established literature on product purchase behavior in France. However, because many of AMC's research questions are very specific, researchers know that they will not be able to answer all their questions from secondary sources; they will need to collect primary data as well. To this end, as part of its research design, AMC decides to conduct a large-scale survey among car consumers in France. This involves constructing a questionnaire that contains questions assessing the issues that AMC seeks to address. Researchers devise a collection of questions that aim to measure constructs related to car buyer behavior, such as "attitude toward American cars," the "meaning of car ownership," and car-related "values" of French consumers. Responses regarding such constructs can vary substantially from country to country.

When formulating some of the survey questions, AMC finds it can use questions and construct measures that it created for similar surveys in the United States. For other questions, AMC consults resources in the market research literature, such as the *Handbook of Marketing Scales* (Bearden & Netemeyer, 1999). The *Handbook* contains numerous measurement scales used by researchers in other studies. For still other survey topics, AMC finds it must create *new* questions, to assess issues highly specific to car consumption in France. In order to create new scales, managers decide to perform exploratory research in France, by conducting interviews with typical French car consumers, to ascertain how best to create the new measurement scales they need. All survey questions must be in the French language, and the survey must be conducted in a manner that best suits typical French consumers. Consequently, AMC hires a French market research firm to translate the questionnaire and perform the research in France. The research firm will *back-translate* the resulting questionnaire, and perform other checks to ensure that representativeness, reliability, and validity, as well as translation, and measurement equivalence, are achieved.

Data Collection

The collected data must be of sufficient quality and specificity to address the research questions identified in Step 1. AMC initially collects secondary data from established literature on product purchase behavior in France. Researchers obtain this data from libraries, government sources, and via the Internet. In addition, AMC buys a few "off-the-shelf" market surveys regarding France's car market from several professional market research firms. Consistent with the research design determined in the previous step, AMC also seeks primary data by conducting a survey of car consumers in France.

To collect the primary data, AMC first selects an appropriate sample, or sampling frame, for its survey. The sampling frame defines the population of consumers in France who will be targeted with the survey. Choosing an appropriate sampling frame, representative of likely Cruiser buyers, helps to ensure external validity. In this way, survey respondents will be representative of the population of likely Cruiser buyers in France. Accordingly, AMC buys a list from a French market research firm of the names and contact information of 38,000 French people who have purchased an economy car in France in the last 3 years. The list also contains details on each person's income level, family size, and other demographic variables. Although eventually aiming to sell hundreds of thousands of cars in France, AMC will sample just 10,000 car buyers drawn at random from the list. On the questionnaire, AMC asks a series of questions that will help to identify consumers most inclined to buy cars. Based on this procedure, researchers will be able to identify respondents who are representative of the likely population of eventual Cruiser car buyers in France.

AMC knows that perhaps only about 2,000 of the group of 10,000 will actually respond to its survey—that is, a response rate of roughly 20%. But by following rigorous statistical procedures, this level of response will be sufficient to obtain reliable and valid results on AMC's survey.

According to sampling theory, researchers can draw conclusions from re-sponses received from only a small percentage of the target population. As long as AMC researchers ensure that the sampled consumers are repre-sentative of the population of likely Cruiser buyers, the firm will be able to ensure that findings from the survey are reasonably accurate.

In general, it is good research practice to account for the types of er-rors in sampling procedure that might confound eventual findings. Dis-cussion on these sampling maladies—such as frame, sampling, and non-response errors—is beyond the scope of this book. We recommend that the reader refer to any statistics or marketing research textbook for such a discussion.

Analysis and Interpretation of Results

AMC's next task is to analyze and interpret the data collected in the previous stage. The first step here involves ensuring that the data are complete and accurate. There are many causes of flawed data. For example, respondents to a survey may not have completed the entire survey, the data may not have been recorded or entered properly, or a respondent may not have answered some survey questions honestly. To address such issues, the re-searcher takes steps to "clean" the data. This typically involves dropping problematic data either in part (e.g., exclude a single question) or in full (e.g., drop an entire survey).

Next the researcher analyzes the data by using a specialized data analysis software package, such as SPSS or SAS. In reality, many firms hire an outside market research firm to perform this analysis. Indeed, many firms hire an outside firm to undertake the entire research process. However, large compa-nies typically acquire the capability to do this type of work in-house.

In data analysis, initially it is good practice to cross-tabulate the data. Cross-tabs show how data are related to one another and give insights about the type of analysis method that the researcher should employ in subsequent phases of the analysis. Once cross-tabs have been performed, the researcher is next likely to use one or both of two techniques: cor-relation analysis and causation analysis. Typically, correlation analysis is performed first, followed by causation analysis. Correlation analysis helps to establish relationships among the variables investigated in the research. For example, using correlation analysis, the researcher could establish the degree of correlation between purchase likelihood of a car and features such as legroom, air conditioning, manual versus automatic transmission, and so forth.

Causation analysis is a deeper, more sophisticated type of analysis. It helps explain the magnitude and direction of the effects of independent variables (e.g., product features) on a dependent variable (e.g., purchase likelihood). For example, by employing causation analysis, the researcher would be able to ascertain whether having an automatic transmission would increase or decrease the likelihood of a French consumer buying a Cruiser. Causation analysis can also reveal the magnitude by which independent variables affect dependent variables. Causation analysis might reveal that having air conditioning is relatively more likely to induce consumer purchase than having an automatic transmission.

A significant task at this stage is establishing reliability and validity in the measures used in AMC's survey. As discussed earlier, these are necessary conditions for establishing that research findings are relatively free from error. The most popular measure of reliability assessment is Cronbach's Alpha. The researcher should seek a Cronbach's Alpha value of at least 70% for each scale used in the survey. In addition, there are numerous methods for establishing the validity of measures in market research, but a discussion of these is beyond the scope of this book. For our purposes, we will assume that reliability and validity have been established.

Reporting the Findings

The final task is to report research findings—from both secondary and primary sources—to management. In the case of small-scale research, communicating results can be quite informal. The marketer may simply draw conclusions from what he or she gleaned from the data analysis. For more serious market research projects, the researcher would prepare a written report that outlines what was researched, summarizes the results, and makes formal recommendations. The report should be comprehensive, easy to understand, and include sound recommendations. When describing the findings, the researcher will typically provide a summary of what has been gathered. For quantitative data, this usually involves creating charts, tables, and other visual representations that summarize the findings. For qualitative data, the researcher should interpret what was learned, typically by coding or summarizing findings into logical grouping categories. The marketer may give an oral presentation in which the research is explained within a slide presentation.

Failed Market Research: An Example

While undertaking market research is critical, findings must be interpreted with great care. If results are inaccurate, or if conclusions are faulty, then incorrect marketing decisions will likely result. Countless firms have made bad decisions based on faulty research.

Take the case of Coca-Cola in the United States, which in response to falling market shares, decided to change the Coke formula and create a new beverage called "New Coke" ("Coca-Cola Co. to bring," 1985; "Coke's brand-loyalty," 1985; Dubow & Childs, 1998; Hartley, 1998). Management's decision was based on research that revealed that people preferred the taste of Pepsi, Coke's archrival. Research also suggested that few people would miss the old Coke. Taste tests uncovered a sweeter formula that consumers preferred over both the old Coke and Pepsi. On April 23, 1985, New Coke was launched and the old Coke was removed from the market. Within 24 hours, most of the U.S. population knew of the change. Initially, millions of people tried New Coke and results looked favorable.

But within two months, Coke received a deluge of negative press and unhappy customer comments. The barrage of negative response was unexpected. Thousands of loyal Coke customers sent disapproving messages to Coke headquarters in Atlanta.

Activists laid plans to file a class action lawsuit against Coke. People began stockpiling the old Coke. Some sold it at scalpers' prices. Fiddling with the 99-year-old formula was seen as an affront to patriotic pride. Strangely, in May 1985, market research had revealed that 53% of consumers liked New Coke. But by July, only 30% said that they liked it.

In July 1985, less than 3 months after the launch, Coca-Cola relented, and the old Coke was reinstated. The news spread fast; the change was the lead story on the nightly network newscasts. On Wall Street, the news drove Coca-Cola stock to its highest level in 12 years.

The entire crisis resulted because Coke's market research was deeply flawed. In taste tests, consumers had not been told that by choosing one

Coke, they would lose the other. While taste tests had been conducted with 200,000 people, only about 35,000 involved the specific formula for New Coke. Research had been geared more to the concept than to the actual product. Research designs were insufficient to elicit deep, complex feelings and emotional ties to the old Coke. Coke researchers had failed to properly identify the research problem and to clearly define key constructs in the research process. New Coke was a sweeter formula, which appealed to younger people, but not to older age groups. Subsequent analyses suggested that Coca-Cola had failed to understand how the old Coke had come to represent various patriotic, sentimental, and nostalgic feelings for many consumers. In a twist of human psychology, even people who first accepted New Coke soon reversed opinion and saw it instead as a betrayal of sacred tradition ("Coca-Cola Co. to bring," 1985; "Coke's brand-loyalty," 1985; Dubow & Childs, 1998; Hartley, 1998).

The New Coke episode underscores the critical importance of conducting accurate market research. On its own, market research is insufficient for effective strategic planning. The manager must also integrate his own intuition and judgment with results of analyses. Research by itself is not a solution and does not replace the manager's intuition and skill in decision making. The manager must exercise skill in understanding the nuances of given situations. In conducting research, the manager will acquire a great deal of data and information, all of which must be synthesized into a big picture, leading to superior decision making. Much of market research is more art than science, and hence, success often hinges on employing skilled researchers, with substantial experience and knowledge about the problems and tasks at hand.

APPENDIX A

Internet Sites for Obtaining Secondary Data

There are countless Web sites to assist the market researcher investigating international opportunities. This appendix is a sampling of some of the most useful sites.

General Resources

GlobalEDGE™ (www.globaledge.msu.edu) is the leading knowledge portal for professionals in international business, providing specialized knowledge on countries, cross-border trade, and a wide range of other topics. This portal combines knowledge, insights, statistics, and research findings on international business, and meets the needs of practitioners and students. Specific resources include Global Resources, Country Insights, Knowledge Room, and Diagnostic Tools. GlobalEDGE™ is home to Market Potential Indicators for Emerging Markets, which ranks emerging market countries on various criteria.

The Organization for Economic Cooperation and Development (OECD; www.oecd.org) is a leading resource providing various data on international trade and investment.

The World Bank (www.worldbank.org) provides useful secondary data through guides such as World Development Indicators, World Bank National Business Regulations, World Bank Doing Business Indicators (www.doingbusiness.org/), investment climate data for individual countries, and much more.

The International Monetary Fund (www.imf.org) provides data on financial and economic conditions for most nations.

The World Trade Organization's International Trade Centre (www.intracen.org/index.htm) offers various trade-related data.

The Project on Human Development at Boston University (human development.bu.edu/) tracks numerous economic, social, and political indicators for individual countries.

Economist Country Briefings (www.economist.com/countries/) provide economic forecasts for most countries.

A. T. Kearney (www.atkearney.com) is a private consultancy that publishes the Foreign Direct Investment Confidence Index, Global Services Location Index, and Global Services Location Index.

U.S. Government Resources

The U.S. Department of Commerce (www.doc.gov) provides much useful data on exporting opportunities (www.export.gov and www.trade .gov).

The National Trade Data Bank (www.stat-usa.gov) contains tens of thousands of documents, reports, and other data from various federal agencies of the U.S. government.

The U.S. Commercial Service Market Research Library (www.export .gov/mrktresearch/index.asp) is a portal linked to various information on international business topics.

The CIA World Factbook (www.cia.gov/cia/publications/factbook/) provides summary information on all countries, such as demographic, economic, political, and technological data.

The U.S. Commercial Service annually publishes a Country Commercial Guide for most countries, explaining in great detail how to do business in each location. The easiest way to find the guide is to enter "country commercial guide [country name]" into the search field at Google (www.google.com) or Ask.com.

United Nations Resources

The United Nations (www.un.org and www.comtrade.un.org/db/) provides various types of statistics, including their Statistical Yearbook of the United Nations.

The United Nations Conference on Trade and Development (UNCTAD; www.unctad.org) collects substantial data on trade topics.

The statistical tables in the Human Development Report, published annually by the United Nations Development Program (UNDP; www .undp.org), reveal the state of human development worldwide.

Specific Country and Region Sites

Leading exemplars include the following:

- International Trade Canada (www.infoexport.gc.ca)
- The Department of Foreign Affairs and Trade in Australia (www .austrade.gov.au)
- The Japan External Trade Organization (JETRO; www.jetro .go.jp)
- The European Union (europa.eu.int; www.eurunion.org)

Political, Legal, and Corruption Conditions Abroad

Transparency International (www.transparency.org) is an independent organization that publishes the annual Corruption Perceptions Index, which ranks the level of corruption in more than 150 countries.

Freedom House (www.freedomhouse.org) is a nongovernmental organization that assesses the level of government accountability, the rule of law, and freedoms of expression and belief in countries worldwide.

The Heritage Foundation (www.heritage.org) annually publishes the Index of Economic Freedom, which measures levels of economic freedom and government intervention in countries worldwide.

The International Intellectual Property Alliance (www.iipa.com) and the Office of the U.S. Trade Representative (www.ustr.gov) report on protection of patents and other intellectual property around the world.

Information on Culture

The Area Studies Web site (www.psr.keele.ac.uk/area.htm) reports on cultural factors in various countries.

Culturegrams (www.culturegrams.com) provide detailed information on culture in numerous countries.

Information on living and working in various countries is available at www.livingabroad.com.

The Hofstede Resource Center (www.geert-hofstede.com) provides detailed information on country-level cultures around the world.

Tariffs and Trade Barriers

Harmonized codes for all manner of products can be accessed at www .census.gov/foreign-trade/schedules/b/index.html. It is necessary to look up the harmonized codes, identifying numbers, of individual products in order to find out the tariffs that firms must pay when exporting them.

After learning the harmonized code, the tariffs on individual products can be found at the Harmonized Tariff Schedule of the United States (www.usitc.gov/tata/hts/bychapter/index.htm).

To look up the tariffs for Australia, Canada, Hong Kong, New Zealand, and other countries around the Pacific Rim, see www.apectariff .org/tdb.cgi.

Labor and Other Factor Conditions Abroad

The U.S. Department of Labor Bureau of Labor Statistics (www.bls.gov/ fls/home.htm) provides international comparisons of hourly compensation costs, productivity, and consumer prices for various countries.

The International Labor Organization (www.ilo.org) and their International Labour Office database (laborsta.ilo.org) offer data on work hours, wages, consumer price indices, labor union strikes, and lockouts in various nations.

The Organisation for Economic Development and Cooperation (www.oecd.org) provides data on labor and productivity worldwide.

Travel and Living Conditions Abroad

The U.S. Department of State (travel.state.gov/travel) provides Consular Information Sheets, which include information on safety, security, crime, medical facilities, and travel warnings for every country.

Mercer (www.mercer.com), a consulting firm, provides the "Top 50 Rankings for Quality of Living" for expatriates and others thinking of moving to countries around the world.

The U.S. Department of State (www.state.gov and aoprals.state.gov/) provides relative cost of living information for most countries around the world.

Google (www.google.com) can be used to research conditions in cities worldwide, regarding quality of life, major attractions, business environment, and culture. Simply enter the city name into a Google search.

For climate data, www.worldclimate.com and www.weather.com provide records on all major cities worldwide.

Assessing Company Readiness to Internationalize

CORE™ (Company Readiness to Export; www.globalEDGE.msu.edu) is an expert system that helps companies analyze their ability to internationalize. By answering a series of questions, the firm can determine its strengths and weaknesses for undertaking any international venture.

Resources Available at a Typical Library

In addition to information available on the Internet, major libraries are home to various resources, such as the following:

Exporter's Encyclopedia (Dun and Bradstreet, updated regularly) addresses the essentials for how to export to most countries, including marketing data and distribution.

Doing Business in Asia (Lexington Books, updated regularly) is typical of many "doing business in" guides on countries and regions worldwide.

APPENDIX B

Developing an International Business Plan*

Once management has decided to sell its offerings abroad, it is critical to develop an international business plan. The plan helps to develop the broad understanding and consensus needed among top managers on conditions in a given foreign market, as well as company goals, objectives, capabilities, and constraints. The plan should account for important facts and goals, set forth time schedules for implementation, and mark milestones so the degree of venture success can be measured. All personnel involved in the internationalization process should agree to the plan, as they are the ones who will implement it. In this way, the plan helps to motivate key personnel.

Take, for example, an international business plan developed to launch one or more of the firm's products in a foreign market. A good international business plan seeks to address questions such as the following:

- Which country or countries should we target for sales development?
- What product(s) do we intend to sell in the foreign market? What modifications, if any, must be made to adapt it for the market? Should we develop any new products for the market?
- What is the basic customer profile in the target market? What marketing and distribution channels should be used to reach these customers?
- What special challenges pertain to the market (e.g., competitors, cultural differences, trade barriers, etc.), and what strategies should be used to address them?

---

* This section draws extensively from *A Basic Guide to Exporting*, published by the U.S. Department of Commerce (www.usatrade.gov).

- What is the most appropriate price to charge for the product?
- What specific operational steps must be taken in order to enter and succeed in the market?
- What is the timeframe for implementing each element of the plan?
- What personnel and company resources are required for achieving the objectives specified in the plan?
- What will be the cost in time and money for each element?
- How will results be evaluated and used to modify the plan?

The first time that the international business plan is developed, it is usually best to keep it simple, perhaps only a few pages long. This is because important market data and planning elements may not yet be available. The initial planning effort itself gradually generates more information and insight. As the planner learns more about the international venture and the firm's competitive position, the plan will become more detailed and complete. From the start, the plan should be viewed and written as a management tool, not a static document. Objectives in the plan should be compared with actual results to measure the success of different strategies. Management should not hesitate to modify the plan and make it more specific as new information and experience are obtained.

Sample Outline for an International Business Plan

Table of Contents
Executive Summary (one or two pages maximum)
Introduction: Why Our Firm Should Undertake This Venture
Part I—International Business Policy Commitment Statement
Part II—Situation/Background Analysis

> Product or Service
> Operations
> Personnel and Export Organization
> Resources of the Firm
> Industry Structure, Competition, and Demand

Part III—Marketing Component

> Identifying, Evaluating, and Selecting Target Markets

Product Selection and Pricing

Distribution Methods

Terms and Conditions

Internal Organization and Procedures

Sales Goals: Profit and Loss Forecasts

Part IV—Tactics: Action Steps

Primary Target Countries

Secondary Target Countries

Indirect Marketing Efforts

Part V—Budget

Pro Forma Financial Statements

Part VI—Implementation Schedule

Follow-up

Periodic Operational and Management Review (Measuring Results Against Plan)

Addenda: Background Data on Target Countries and Market

Basic Market Statistics: Historical and Projected

Background Facts

Competitive Environment

References

Amine, L. S., & Cavusgil, S. T. (1986). Demand estimation in the developing country environment: Difficulties, techniques and examples. *Journal of the Market Research Society, 28,* 43–65.

Arnould, E., Price, L., & Zinkhan, G. (2002). *Consumers.* Burr Ridge, IL: McGraw-Hill/Irwin.

As good as it gets: Special report Samsung Electronics. (2005, January 13). *The Economist,* 64–66.

Bearden, W., & Netemeyer, R. (1999). *Handbook of marketing scales: Multi-item measures for marketing and consumer behavior research.* Thousand Oaks, CA: Sage.

Cavusgil, S. T. (1985, November–December). Guidelines for export market research. *Business Horizons, 28,* 27–33.

Cavusgil, S. T. (1997, January–February). Measuring the potential of emerging markets: An indexing approach. *Business Horizons, 40,* 87–91.

Cavusgil, S. T., Knight, G., & Riesenberger, J. (2008) *International business* (1st ed.). Upper Saddle River, NJ: Prentice Hall.

Coca-Cola Co. to bring back its old Coke. (1985, July 11). *Wall Street Journal,* p. 1.

Coke's brand-loyalty lesson. (1985, August 5). *Fortune,* 44.

Craig, C. S., & Douglas, S. P. (2005). *International marketing research* (3rd ed.). New York: John Wiley and Sons.

Crocker, G., & Tay, Y.-C. (2004). What it takes to create a successful brand. *The China Business Review, 31*(4), 10–16.

Day, G., & Montgomery, D. (1999). Charting new directions for marketing. *Journal of Marketing, 63*(3), 3–14.

de Jong, M., Steenkamp, J., Fox, J., & Baumgartner, H. (2008). Using item response theory to measure extreme response style in marketing research: A global investigation. *Journal of Marketing Research, 45*(1), 104–115.

Dubow, J., & Childs, N. (1998). New Coke, mixture perception and the flavor balance hypothesis. *Journal of Business Research, 43*(3), 147–155.

Edy, C. (1999, June). The Olympics of marketing. *American Demographics,* 47–48.

Fishbein, M., & Ajzen, I. (1975). *Belief, attitude, intention and behavior.* Reading, MA: Addison-Wesley.

Gerbing, D., & Anderson, J. (1988). An updated paradigm for scale development incorporating unidimensionality and its assessment. *Journal of Marketing Research, 25*(2), 186–192.

globalEDGE™. (2005). *Market potential indicators for emerging markets.* Retrieved August 7, 2008, from http://ciber.bus.msu.edu/publicat/mktptind.htm

Gutman, J. (1982). A means-end chain model based on consumer categorization processes. *Journal of Marketing, 46*(2), 60–72.

Gutman, J. (1984). Analyzing consumer orientations toward beverages through means-end chain analysis. *Psychology & Marketing, 1*(3/4), 23–43.

Hartley, R. (1998). *Marketing mistakes and successes.* New York: John Wiley and Sons.

Hofstede, G. (1980). *Culture's consequences: International differences in work-related values.* Beverly Hills, CA: Sage.

Hofstede, G. (2001). *Culture's consequences: Comparing values, behaviors, institutions, and organizations across nations.* Thousand Oaks, CA: Sage.

Honomichl, J. (2006, August 15). Honomichl global top 25. *Marketing News,* 20.

House, R., Hanges, P., Javidan, M., Dorfman, P., & Gupta, V. (2004). *Culture, leadership, and organizations: The GLOBE study of 62 societies.* Thousand Oaks, CA: Sage.

Inglehart, R. (1997). *Modernization and postmodernization: Cultural, economic, and political change in 43 societies.* Princeton, NJ: Princeton University Press.

Kahle, L. (1983). *Social values and social change.* New York: Praeger.

Kamakura, W., & Novak, T. (1992). Value-system segmentation: Exploring the meaning of LOV. *Journal of Consumer Research, 19*(1), 119–132.

Kiley, D. (2007, August 6). The top 100 global brands. *Business Week,* 59–64.

Lee, G., & Hall, N. (2004, June). Brand strategy briefing: The 15 global hot buttons. *Brand Strategy,* 58.

Lim, J., Sharkey, T., & Kim, K. (1996). Competitive environmental scanning and export involvement: An initial inquiry. *International Marketing Review, 13*(1), 65–80.

Markus, H., & Kitayama, S. (1991). Culture and self: Implications for cognition, emotion, and motivation. *Psychological Review, 98,* 224–253.

Mitchell, A. (1983). *The nine American lifestyles: Who we are and where we're going.* New York: Macmillan.

Netemeyer, R., Bearden, W., & Sharma, S. (2003). *Scaling procedures: Issues and applications.* Thousand Oaks, CA: Sage.

Ng, D. (2004, May). Banks think globally but price locally. *USBanker,* 14.

Porter, M. (1990). *The competitive advantage of nations.* New York: Free Press.

Reynolds, T., & Gutman, J. (1988). Laddering theory, method, analysis, and interpretation. *Journal of Advertising Research, 28*(1), 11–31.

Rokeach, M. (1973). *The nature of human values.* New York: Free Press.

Roper Starch Worldwide. (2000, October). The 3-D consumer: Nationality and lifestage values. *American Demographics,* s5–s17.

Schwartz, S. (1992). Universals in the content and structure of values: Theory and empirical tests in 20 countries. In M. Zanna (Ed.), *Advances in experimental social psychology* (Vol. 25, pp. 1–65). New York: Academic Press.

Schwartz, S., & Bilsky, W. (1987). Toward a universal psychological structure of human values. *Journal of Personality and Social Psychology, 53*(3), 550–562.

Schwartz, S., & Bilsky, W. (1990). Toward a theory of the universal content and structure of values: Extensions and cross-cultural replications. *Journal of Personality and Social Psychology, 58*(5), 878–890.

Sharma, S., Shimp, T., & Shin, J. (1995). Consumer ethnocentrism: A test of antecedents and moderators. *Journal of the Academy of Marketing Science, 23*(1), 26–37.

Shimp, T., & Sharma, S. (1987). Consumer ethnocentrism: Construction and validation of the CETSCALE. *Journal of Marketing Research, 24*(3), 280–289.

Steenkamp, J., ter Hofstede, F., & Wedel, M. (1999). A cross-national investigation into the individual and national cultural antecedents of consumer innovativeness. *Journal of Marketing, 63*(2), 55–69.

Storey, R., & Robinson, D. (2004). *Vietnam.* Oakland, CA: Lonely Planet.

UNCTAD. (2006). *World investment report 2006.* New York: United Nations Conference on Trade and Development.

U.S. Department of Commerce. (1992). *A basic guide to exporting.* Washington, DC: U.S. Government Printing Office.

VW's American road trip. (2006, January 4). *Wall Street Journal,* p. B1.

Wedel, M., & Kamakura, W. (2000). *Market segmentation: Conceptual and methodological foundations.* Boston: Kluwer Academic.

Index

Page numbers followed by *t* and *f* refer to tables and figures, respectively.

CPSIA information can be obtained at www.ICGtesting.com
Printed in the USA
LVOW132147020812

292758LV00009B/85/P